# INDIA:

ITS

HISTORY, CLIMATE, PRODUCTIONS,

AND

FIELD SPORTS

# INDIA:

ITS

HISTORY, CLIMATE, PRODUCTIONS,

AND

FIELD SPORTS;

WITH NOTICES OF

**EUROPEAN LIFE AND MANNERS,**

AND OF THE VARIOUS

**TRAVELLING ROUTES**

**J. H. STOCQUELER**

GYAN

*Published by*

Gyan Publishing House
5, Ansari Road
Daryaganj, New Delhi-110002
Phone: 011-47034999, 9811692060
E-mail: books@gyanbooks.com

*Distribution Network*
gyanbooks.com
India, USA, Canada, UK, Australia, France



ISBN: 978-81-212-8628-2 (PB)
First Published, 1853

2nd Impression 2023

*Printed at:* Gyan Press, Delhi.



**INDIA: ITS HISTORY, CLIMATE, PRODUCTIONS, AND FIELD SPORTS**
Author: J. H. STOCQUELER

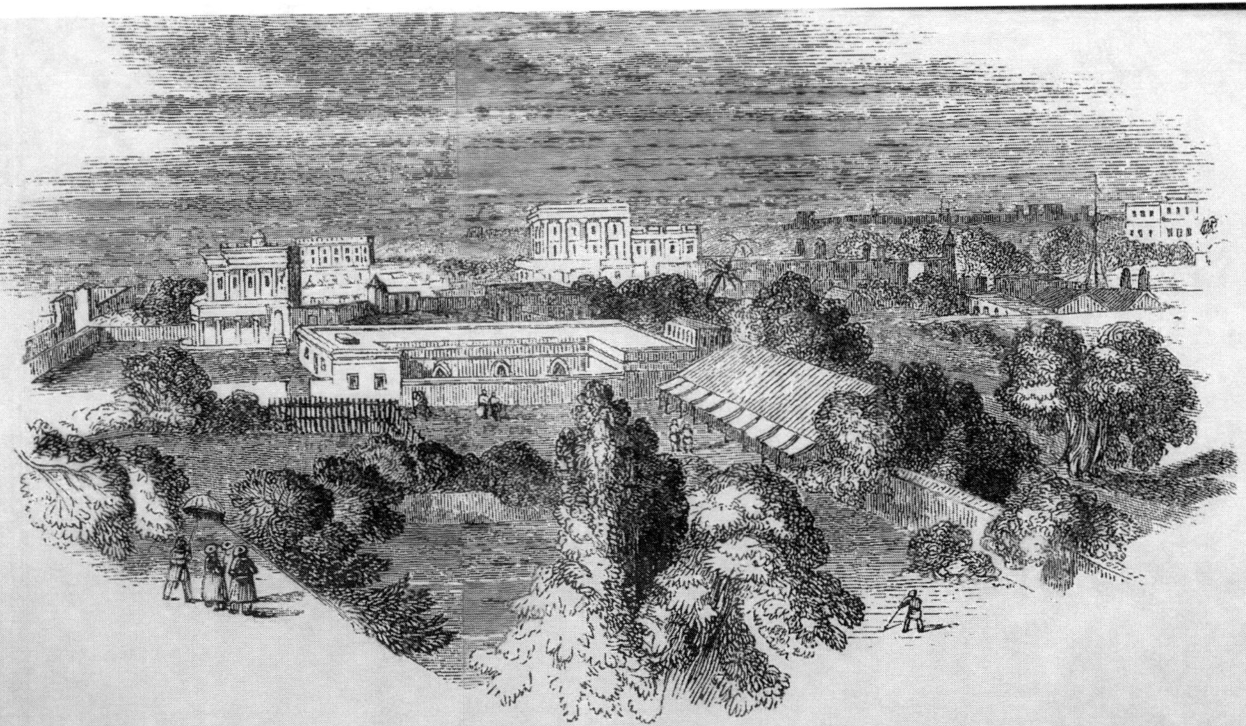

View of Calcutta.

# INDIA:

ITS

# HISTORY, CLIMATE, PRODUCTIONS,

AND

# FIELD SPORTS;

WITH NOTICES OF

## EUROPEAN LIFE AND MANNERS,

AND OF THE VARIOUS

## TRAVELLING ROUTES.

BY

J. H. STOCQUELER,

AUTHOR OF THE "ORIENTAL INTERPRETER."

*With Illustrations.*

---

EIGHTH THOUSAND.

---

LONDON:

GEORGE ROUTLEDGE AND CO.,

FARRINGDON STREET.

1854.

# PREFACE.

In this little volume an attempt has been made to condense and concentrate all the information regarding the British empire in the East, which is essential to the masses. At a moment when the Act of Parliament under which the East India Company have governed India is expiring, and a new Act, paving the way for the transfer of India to the Crown of England, is passing through the legislature, it behoves every Englishman to make himself acquainted with a country of so vast an extent, and so interesting a character, upon national grounds alone. The day is not remote when India will cease to be a "close borough"—patronage must give way to competition, and the man of talent and energy will find the road to preferment as open to him and to his children, as it has hitherto exclusively been to the offspring and connections of the Directors of the East India Company. Very much has been written about India by numerous able pens. Her history, government, natural productions, commerce, geography, ethnology,—her religions, temples, antiquities, scenery,—the manners and customs of the manifold tribes contained in her wide continent and adjacent islands—occupy libraries of volumes, from the ponderous folio to the thick octavo, but nowhere can access be obtained to a compendium of knowledge on these points. In an age when the claims upon our time are so numerous, that very little attention can be bestowed on any single subject by ordinary readers, an endeavour to present a general epitome of the contents of all the works that have been published appears to be particularly called for; and although the author of the following rapid sketch cannot expect to have satisfied curiosity upon all points, he hopes at least to have succeeded in conveying a general notion of "India," and a correct idea of the routes to that country, and the expenses of the voyage.

# CONTENTS.

## CHAPTER I.

### INDIA AND HER HISTORY.

Geographical sketch—The early Hindoo settlers—Alexander's invasion—The Mahomedan conquerors—Discovery of the route to India round the Cape of Good Hope—The settlement of Europeans in India—Dupleix' views of French empire—Clive—The progress of conquest—The Mahrattas, Burmah, The Punjaub . . . . . . . . page 1

## CHAPTER II.

### THE GOVERNMENT OF INDIA.

Early Government—Establishment of the Board of Control—The East India Direction—The Governmental Divisions of India—The Bengal, Madras, and Bombay Presidencies—The Native States—The Civil administration—The Army of India—The Indian Navy—Furloughs, Half-pay, Retirements, &c. . . . . . . . page 14

## CHAPTER III.

### THE ROUTES TO INDIA.

Sea voyage—The expense—The necessary equipment—Sailing ships—Screw steamers—The overland route—The steamers of the Peninsular and Oriental Company—The cost and the equipment . . . . . . . page 32

## CHAPTER IV.

### THE EMIGRANT TO INDIA.

The European population of India—Its character and extent—Advice to emigrants—Equipment for such persons page 42

## CHAPTER V.

### EUROPEAN LIFE IN INDIA.

European life in India—The kind of houses required—Method of furnishing—Domestics—Articles of life—Markets—Household expenses—Amusements and resources—Diet—Routine of existence—Literature—Life in the Mofussil—The indigo planter—Life of a lady in India—Children . page 49

## CHAPTER VI.

### TRAVELLING IN INDIA.

The first railway—Boat travelling on the Ganges—The banks of the Hooghly—Dawk—Marching—The necessary preparations and equipment . . . . . . page 72

## CHAPTER VII.

### THE VEGETABLE PRODUCTIONS OF INDIA.

The Banian tree—Ganesha—The Peepul—General belief—The Sissoo — The Sygwam—The Talipot, its uses— The Cocoa-nut, invaluable to the native — Traditions of the mango grove . . . . . . . . . page 90

## CHAPTER VIII.

### COMMERCE, COINS, WEIGHTS, MEASURES, ETC.

Articles of export and import—The carrying trade—Exchange —Bullion—The system of weights—The Banyan—Docks — Commercial Office Establishments — The shipping for a twelvemonth . . . . . . . . page 99

## CHAPTER IX.

### THE FRUITS OF INDIA.

The Pine-apple—The Custard-apple—The Mango—The Egg-plum—The Pomegranate — The Melon — The Guava—The Plantain—The Pumplenose—The Papaya—The Loquat — The Jack—The Leechee, &c. . . . . . page 109

## CHAPTER X.

### THE CLIMATE OF INDIA.

General range of the thermometer — Bengal, Madras, and Bombay — Remedies for heat — Diseases of India — Hill stations . . . . . . . . . . page 124

## CHAPTER XI.

### THE WILD SPORTS OF INDIA.

Jackall hunting—Boar hunting—Tiger hunting—The man tiger—The Nepaul Terai—Elephant hunting—Bear hunting—Deer stalking . . . . . . . . . page 129

## CHAPTER XII.

### RELIGIOUS CEREMONIES, CREEDS, ETC.

The Brahminical religion—The Doorga Poojah—The Nautch—Hindoo music—The Churuk Poojah—Juggernat'h—The Suttee—The Mohurrum—The Buckra Eade—The Bhearer . . . . . . . . . page 143

## CHAPTER XIII.

### ARCHITECTURE, TEMPLES, MONUMENTAL REMAINS, ETC.

The cave temples—The river temples—The character of Hindoo sculpture—Futtehpore Sikri—Deeg—Secundra—Tomb of Hoomaioon—Agra—The Taj Mahal—Lucknow, &c. page 170

## CHAPTER XIV.

### THE CHIEF TOWNS OF INDIA.

Calcutta, Madras, and Bombay—Delhi—The Great Mogul—Agra—Lucknow—Benares—Hyderabad . . page 185

## CHAPTER XV.

### CEYLON.

Productions—Colombo—Trincomalee—Point de Galle—Kandy—Climate—Population . . . . . . page 202

# INDIA.

---

## CHAPTER I.

### INDIA, AND HER HISTORY.

*Geographical sketch—The early Hindoo settlers—Alexander's invasion—The Mahomedan conquerors—Discovery of the route to India round the Cape of Good Hope—The settlement of Europeans in India—Dupleix' views of French empire—Clive—The progress of conquest—The Mahrattas, Burmah, the Punjaub.*

INDIA! To the reader of history, and the student of human nature, what varied associations present themselves in that single word! Magnificent enterprises, incomparable heroism, unequalled sagacity, incredible cruelty, horrible superstition, wonderful perseverance, grandeur of conception, multiplied instances of the loftiest efforts and the most abject degradation of humanity—the meeting at once of the extremities of the sublime and the contemptible; these, and a thousand other objects, strike the mind when the past history and the present condition of British India are forced upon consideration. In no part of the world are we presented with so striking a proof of the influence of moral over brute force, or of the decay of

Paganism in the presence of healthful Christian exercise. Nowhere else do we behold the simple trader rising into the most powerful ruler; millions of acres of waste land and jungle rescued from the marauder and the tiger, and converted into fertile lands and the abodes of peace and industry; an agglomeration of nations, covering a vast extent of country, acknowledging the supremacy of a handful of islanders, whose seat of government is five thousand miles away! India is a marvellous problem, a phenomenon which puzzles the philosopher, while it charms the philanthropist. To the whole world its position is a mystery —to Englishmen a subject of the deepest interest and the most lively solicitude.

The story of the occupation and mastery of India by the English is soon told, and forms an unavoidable prelude to the description we propose to give of the country generally, and the means of access to its shores. But first let us glance at the geography of the land of which we intend to treat.

British India is comprehended in a continent extending north to south from Cape Comorin, in lat. 8° N., and long. 77° E., to the Himalaya chain. On the west it is bounded by the Indian Ocean; on the east by the Bay of Bengal. But even upon the western shores of that bay England holds possessions, and governs multitudes; for a considerable portion of what was once the Burmese empire now acknowledges our sway. The Tenasserim coast, the island of Pulo Penang (now called Prince of Wales's Island), Malacca, and the island of Singapore, are British settlements. The once independent kingdom of Pegu has been annexed to the dominions of the British crown, and even a nook in China and a point in Borneo are occupied by us in virtue of treaties. To secure a free passage in and out of the Red Sea, the little town and anchorage of Aden, in the straits of Babelmandeb, have been ceded to us; and possibly at this moment the successes of our army in Burmah may be extending our possessions to the very capital of Ava. Immediately south of the peninsula of India is the island of Ceylon, which is likewise British territory; and thus upon some part of every state on the shores of the eastern hemisphere the English ensign flutters in the breeze, and is hailed as the type of civilization and the earnest of protection to all within its influence who suffer from oppression.

The early history of India is perhaps more perplexing than that of any other country which boasts of an ancient civilization. Employing no dates, or clues to dates, in their temples and monuments, perpetuating no rulers but those who owned a (fabulous) divine origin, the people have furnished to posterity no starting point in the story of their origin upon which a rational mind can place the smallest reliance. All that is really ascertainable is, that two thousand years ago they had a religion "less disgraced by idolatrous worship than most of those which prevailed in early times." They had a despotic government, restricted, however, by law, institutions, and religion; a code of laws, in many respects wise and rational, and adapted to a great variety of relations which could not have existed excepting in an advanced state of social organization. They had "a copious and cultivated language, and an extensive and diversified literature; they had made great progress in the mathematical sciences; they speculated profoundly on the mysteries of men and nature; and they had acquired remarkable proficiency in many of the ornamental and useful arts of life. In short, whatever defects may be justly attributed to their religion, their government, their laws, their literature, their sciences, their arts, as contrasted with the same proofs of civilization in modern Europe, the Hindoos were in all these respects quite as civilized as any of the most civilized nations of the ancient world, and in as early times as any of which records or traditions remain."*

From the wonderful influence which Brahminism has exercised in all times over Hindostan, and the vast remains of temples whose antiquity it is impossible to determine, the inference drawn by historians and antiquarians is, that the first foreign settlers in India were a colony of priests from some of the countries west of the Indus; that the whole country was, until their advent, one immense jungle, inhabited by a race of savages no further removed from wild beasts than are the Bosjesmans of Africa. The Brahmins introduced a religion, and gradually spreading themselves in a southerly direction, founded the kingdom of Oude, which, according to their Puranas or sacred books, in which all the traditions (miscalled history) of the Hindoos are written, was the birthplace of the dynasties of the sun and moon. Both of these planets, thus personified, are said to have issued originally from Brahma, or the supreme being, through his sons the patriarchs Daksha and Atri.

It were a waste of time to follow tradition through all its absurdities and exaggerations from such a point. Let it suffice that the Brahminical religion, aided by the persecution of fire and sword, gradually extended its influence over the minds of the Mlechas or original barbarians of the country, and at length reached the most southerly point of the continent, and even the island of Ceylon, spreading civilization, and partially converting forests into smiling plains. The people of the coasts, acquiring the science of navigation and ship-building — how or when, no records show — gradually opened a communication by sea with other countries; and discovering within the bosom of their

* Professor H. H. Wilson.

own fertile lands various precious metals, with which they decorated their persons or manufactured drinking and other vessels, soon became objects of attraction to their neighbours. Egypt and Assyria were in very early times in communication with India; but it is not until Alexander the Macedonian penetrates Persia, Affghanistan, and the Punjaub, to the river Hyphasis (the modern Beeas), that we obtain any authentic account of the country. This was 325 years before Christ. From that time onwards we lose trace of any connection between India and the nations west of the river Indus, until we find the Saracens, who had conquered Persia, recruiting their forces from among the wild tribes of Turks and Tartars—who, like the Goths, Vandals and Huns, had always a hankering after the south—and then invading India. "After the conversion of the Affghans to Mahomedanism," says Dr. Cooke Taylor, "which took place in less than half a century from the first promulgation of that religion, frequent incursions were made into the territories of the Hindoos; avarice and bigotry combined to stimulate the marauders to cruelty, for they regarded their victims as at once the most wealthy and the most obstinate of idolators." This was 1,100 years ago, or at the beginning of the eighth century since the birth of our Lord. The tide of Mahomedan conquest having once set in an easterly direction, it continued incessantly; and although much stout resistance appears to have been offered to the successive invaders, whether Affghans or Tartars, they seem by the commencement of the sixteenth century to have established their dominion over the whole of the Indian continent, governing in the south by deputy, and allowing Hindoo sovereigns to retain their possessions only on the condition of their paying heavy tribute.

Although, according to Herodotus, the route round the Cape to India had been effected three thousand seven hundred years ago by the Egyptians, under the government of Pharoah Necho II., the produce of India only reached Europe during the thirteenth and fourteenth centuries of the Christian era through the Persian and Arabian gulfs; for the Venetians and Genoese, even if they were aware of any other route than those, carefully kept it a secret from the rest of the world, and for a long time enjoyed a monopoly of the trade. But the wealth of the Italian republics arising out of this monopoly at length awakened the cupidity and jealousy of other nations, and the observation of travellers having led men to reflect on the geographical consequences resulting from the spherical figure of the earth, an idea arose (out of a false calculation of the longitude of Asia), that India might be reached by a voyage from the coasts of Europe in a westerly direction. Columbus first received this impression, and its results are well known to the reader. Much about the same time John II., the King of Portugal, commanded Bartholomew Diaz to ascertain whether the coast of Africa was, as Ptolemy had previously affirmed, terminated by land which stretched to the west, or whether any opening to the east lay along that coast in its southerly direction. The description of Diaz's voyage is graphically told in the following passage from the "Edinburgh Cabinet Library":—"John placed three vessels under the command of Bartholomew Diaz, whom he strictly enjoined, if possible, to pass the southern boundary of the continent; and this officer having arrived at the mouth of the Congo by a course now easy and ascertained, began from that point his career of discovery. He adopted the odd contrivance of carrying with him four negro damsels well clothed, and furnished with gold and silver ornaments, toys and spices, whom he landed at different points of the coast, that they might spread brilliant reports of the wealth and power of the Portuguese.

He gave names, as he went along, to remarkable bays and capes, and at St. Jago, 120 leagues beyond the Congo, erected a pillar of stone to denote at once the dominion of the King and the Cross. He passed successively the Bays of the Landing, of Isles, and of Windings, the last named being given on account of the many changes of course which during five days the sinuosities of the coast, and adverse gales, obliged him to make. The weather continuing stormy, drove him from the land in a southern direction, where his frail barks seemed scarcely fitted to live amid the tempestuous seas by which they were surrounded. After a voyage, too, along the burning shores of Guinea, the Portuguese felt intensely the cold blasts of the Antarctic seas. They considered themselves as lost; when, after thirteen days, the tempest having abated, they sought, by steering eastward, to regain the land; but they were already beyond the farthest point of Africa, and saw nothing before them except the unbounded ocean. Surprised and bewildered they turned towards the north, and at length reached the coast at a point which proved to be beyond the Cape of Good Hope. They called it the 'Bay of Cows,' from the large herds seen feeding, but which the natives immediately drove into the interior. Diaz steered onwards till he came to a small island, where he planted another pillar or ensign of dominion. A general murmur, however, now arose among his exhausted and dispirited crew. They urged that they had already discovered enough land for one voyage, having sailed over more sea than had been traversed by any former expedition; that their vessel was shattered and their provisions drawing to a close; and finally, that the coast having been left running north and south, and now found running west and east, there must intervene some remarkable cape, the discovery of which would give lustre to their voyage homeward.

Diaz then called a council of his principal officers, who all agreed in the necessity of returning. The commander yielded, it is said, with deep reluctance, and parted from the island where he had planted his last ensign as a father parts from an exiled son. The Portuguese had not sailed far westward when they came in view of that mighty promontory which had been vainly sought for so many ages, constituting, as it were, the boundary between two worlds. The commodore, from the storms he had endured in doubling it, named it the Cape of Tempests; but on his return, the king, animated by a more sanguine spirit, bestowed the appellation, which it has ever since retained, of the Cape of Good Hope."

The way thus opened to India by the Portuguese was soon afterwards tracked by the Dutch, the English, the Spaniards, and the French. All commenced their operations upon the coast of India as simple traders who had formed themselves into companies, for the double purpose of obtaining the command of a larger amount of capital and enjoying the protection of their respective sovereigns, who were by no means indifferent to enterprises which contributed to augment the wealth and enhance the political importance of the nations. It was in the year 1600 that Queen Elizabeth granted the first charter to the East India Company. From that time until near the middle of the eighteenth century we were content to possess factories upon the Malabar and Coromandel coasts, and to exist as merchants by sufferance. As long as the nabobs and rajahs—the viceroys of the Great Mogul or Emperor of Delhi, who ruled India—found their account in exactions in the shape of duty, they tolerated the visitors, and the Europeans bore with the arrogance of the delegate governors for the sake of the advantages to be reaped from a commerce in cottons and silks, drugs and spices, gold dust and elephants' tusks.

Gradually, as the settlements of the French and English increased in number, the factors sought permission to introduce small detachments of European troops for the protection of their property; and to these they added a handful of sepoys, or native soldiers, trained and partially costumed after the European manner.

By the year 1747, one Dupleix, a French commandant, had conceived the idea of establishing an independent empire in India. He was an unscrupulous man, of great courage and ambition—one of those who are produced every half-century to astound the world by their successes, and ultimately to sink into insignificance. Conscious of his inability to achieve any great objects single-handed, he began by sowing dissensions among the nabobs in his neighbourhood. The distance at which these viceroys were placed from Delhi made them almost irresponsible, and they acted more like independent sovereigns than delegates from a greater potentate. A vacancy in the viceroyalty, or Nizamut of the Deccan, gave rise to disputes about the succession, and led the rival pretenders to take up arms. Dupleix immediately offered assistance in the shape of French troops and artillery to one of the contending parties—the other threw himself upon the protection of the English, and Major Stringer Lawrence, the English commandant, entered heart and soul into the contest. From this moment began those military operations and political intrigues which eventuated first in the expulsion of the French from India, and gradually led to the entire possession of the country by the English.

To Clive—the brave, the enterprising, and sagacious —we owe the first foundation of British power in the East, and without going into a history, which must be read in all its entirety to enable the reader to come to just conclusions, we may fairly assume that if every part of his conduct was not regulated by the most upright principles, and if some part of his successes was more owing to good fortune than wisdom (for he was strangely eccentric in some respects), it cannot be doubted or denied that he was, from first to last, animated by a noble and unexampled patriotism.

It were impossible, within the limits of this work, to trace the gradual growth of the British empire in India, the result of the combined action of commerce and war, or the rise and progress of the Mahratta States, and the destruction of the confederacy formed by them against the English. The reader who would know how, from simple traders, we have become the mighty masters of the most extensive empire that ever has existed since the downfall of Roman supremacy, must consult the pages of Mill, Orme, Elphinstone, Wilson, and Macfarlane, and the thousand and one lesser volumes which enter into the details of war and the progress of civilization. He would there learn how, in their struggles to maintain supremacy, the native sovereigns and chieftains leagued against us have succumbed to the valour and discipline of small united bodies of troops, headed in battle by daring and sagacious officers; how the infraction of treaties has led to the chastisement of Nabobs and Rajahs, and the confiscation of their territory; how the insolence and violence of the Burmese caused expeditions to be sent to the kingdom of Ava, ending in victory and the appropriation of the land upon the coasts, and the once independent kingdom of Pegu; how the atrocious irruption of the Sikhs into the British dominions was followed by sanguinary campaigns, which terminated in the annexation of the whole of the Punjaub to the Anglo-Indian possessions; how Scinde, by her treachery, became a British province; and how, after the sword had done its work, the arts of peace and the influence of the Gospel were employed to give the newly conquered people assurance of protection, and promote human enlightenment.

Opinions vary as to the strict integrity of all the transactions which have made the East India Company masters of India. According to some writers, wanton aggression, on the part of the English, has been the herald of spoliation; others, perhaps better informed, show that the onus of provocation to war, and the ultimate appropriation of territory, generally lay with the native princes. Perhaps in this, as in other cases, truth lies between the two extremes. One thing, at least, is certain—whether we have come by our empire righteously or unrighteously—whether we have been forced into possessions we did not covet, or have sought quarrels that we might gain by their issue—the natives at large have essentially benefited by the change of masters. We do not, indeed, erect temples to idolatry, nor vast choultries and caravanserais, nor huge tombs, nor lofty fortresses; but we have done our best, amidst enormous difficulties and obstructions, to give the people the benefits of education and of a wholesome administration of justice; we have constructed roads and canals, built bridges, introduced steam navigation, and improved agriculture; we have been tolerant of their prejudices and their various forms of worship; we have encouraged the supercession of empirics by educated practitioners in the healing art; we have respected private property alike in our public and every-day transactions; and we have shown them the way to wealth and preferment by the steady paths which have led Englishmen in all countries to eminence and respect. In proof of the effects of our rule, and the ready way in which the people, however at one time hostile to us and the Christian religion, adapt themselves to our government, the following extract from one of the principal newspapers published in India, describing the condition of our latest conquest, the Punjaub, may be safely offered:—

"Looking at the state of the country politically we

think there is a remarkable opening for the ministers of the Gospel. As perfect peace and good order reign in the whole extent of the Punjaub as in any part of England. We see nothing to deter any prudent, faithful man, from travelling about in all parts, or settling in any one place, and preaching the gospel of salvation fully; and, in doing so, holding up to just condemnation all the false systems by which the people are held bound of Satan. Much more, we think there is not only a wholesome fear, but a just respect, for the Englishman. The Government of the country has done much to establish this state of things. The governing board are well known for their high principles, and their spirit and example pervade all the officers of Government, who seem to have been selected for energy, talent, habits of business, and upright character. The rapidity of the improvements in the country is really wonderful. A few years have done the work of an age in the Punjaub; and the people, feeling perfect security for life and property, and a strong reliance upon the administration of justice, are freed from all petty oppression, and, in the full exercise of industrious pursuits, are not only contented but happy, and, moreover, the general state of European society is good. 'It does one good' (we refer to a private letter) 'to see so many men of talent and rank all intent on their work, and all alive and progressing onward, and sparing no labour of either body or mind to perform their end. Everything here is on the alert. Men are on their Arab horses, and off, at a moment's notice, anywhere, and at a rate that would terrify some in England. Others go out and spend six months at a time in tents, and think nothing of either the hot sun by day or the cold frosts by night, as they travel along administering justice from town to town. They have sometimes to leave a station at a week's notice, and, selling off all, go to a distant part of the country.

And, if men gladly do all these things as soldiers or rulers, surely we ought not to be behind in a better cause. They seem here to have their eyes open to everything that is going on in the whole country, making roads and canals, erecting bridges, settling the revenue, building cantonments, planting trees, and looking into the minutiæ of everything. But we want more men, for the members of the Government are doing all they possibly can to encourage us, and probably there are few countries where such an opening presents itself.'"

# CHAPTER II.

## THE GOVERNMENT OF INDIA.

*Early Government—Establishment of the Board of Control—The East India Direction—The Governmental Divisions of India—The Bengal, Madras, and Bombay Presidencies—The Native States—The Civil administration—The Army of India—The Indian Navy—Furloughs, Half-pay, Retirements, &c.*

For a long time after they had obtained territorial possessions in India, the East India Company ruled without acknowledging any responsibility to the Crown of England. Uncontrolled power, however, begat oppression, and the moral sense of England was outraged between 1770 and 1780 by the receipt of continual representations, that the grossest cruelty and injustice were perpetrated by Englishmen. The enormities charged against the local governors were, of course, exaggerated, and it was difficult to arrive at the truth when distance interposed an impenetrable veil between the actors in the alleged atrocities and their judges; but the immense wealth which some Englishmen who had returned from India displayed, and the arrogant style of life they adopted, had sufficiently excited the jealousy of the aristocracy of this country to induce it to give ready credence to everything that was advanced to the disparagement of Indian "nabobs," as they were called. Constitutional privilege, however, exacted that even the misdeeds imputed to the English lords of the East, should not be summarily dealt with. Official and public inquiry are the necessary preludes to chastisement. Accordingly, at the close of the American war, two committees of the Houses of Parliament sat on Eastern Affairs. "In one Edmund Burke took the lead. The other was under the presidency of the able and versatile Henry Dundas, then Lord-Advocate of Scotland. There was as yet no connection between the Company and either of the great parties in the state. The Ministers had no motive to defend Indian abuses. On the contrary, it was for their interest to show, if possible, that the government and patronage of our Oriental Empire might, with advantage, be transferred to themselves. The votes, therefore, which, in consequence of the reports made by the two committees, were passed by the Commons, breathed the spirit of stern and indignant justice."*

From this time (1784) the government of India was placed under a Board of Control, composed of the King's Ministers, who, in that capacity, bore the title of Commissioners for the Affairs of India, and from that time to the present the system of control has continued. The Home Government thus consists of an East Indian Direction, whose *locale* is Leadenhall-street, and the President of the Board of Control, whose place of business is Cannon Row. The Directors enjoy nearly the whole of the patronage of India, but the higher offices and commands are made in communication with the Ministry, who likewise originate all questions of peace and war, and who

* Macaulay's "Warren Hastings."

possess the power of reversing the acts of the East India Company and the Governments in India, and also of sending out instructions on special matters to the Governor-General without consulting the Directors.

East India Directors are elected by the proprietors of a certain amount of India stock, who seldom trouble themselves about the fitness of the candidates for their favours. Thus, the London interest often prevails over the claims founded on service in India, and we continually witness struggles for a seat in the Direction, terminating in favour of an opulent merchant or banker, a prosperous lawyer, or "eminent brewer." The emoluments of the office of Director are by no means great; the influence which the patronage gives is therefore justly supposed to be the grand motive for the competition. Once elected, a Director retains his power for life, going out of office, however, every four years, to be restored in rotation. The duties which pertain to the office are slight, excepting in the case of the chairman and deputy-chairman, and the select committee, who do all the work. The "chairs" communicate with the President of the Board of Control. There are several secretaries and under-secretaries at the East India House, and as these offices are only conferred upon functionaries who have long held appointments there, it is to be presumed that they are required to be well acquainted with usage and precedent and all the forms of office.

For the purpose of facilitating the government of so vast an empire, India has been divided into three presidencies, or distinct local governments, each under a Governor and a Council. The Governor is the *president* of the Council, whence the title of the gubernatorial division; but one of these governors is also Governor-General of India, and to his supreme authority the others owe obedience in respect to all matters of general concern.

View of Bombay.

The three Presidencies are respectively called the Bombay, Madras, and Bengal.

The Bombay Presidency comprehends the whole of the territority to the westward from Scinde to the vicinity of Goa, north and south, and all that part of the country from the Malabar coast to the interior, which is known as the Deccan, the Concan, Guzerat, and the southern Mahratta country.

The Madras Presidency embraces the Coromandel coast, the country south of the Deccan, to the extreme point of the Indian peninsula, and the territory west of the Coromandel coast, to the boundary of the Bombay presidency.

The Bengal Presidency comprehends the whole of the stations from the entrance of the river Hooghly, north of the Bay of Bengal, to the river Indus. The Himalayan chain, the kingdom of Nepal, are upon its northern and north-eastern limits. West and south it extends to the boundaries of the Bombay and Madras governments. For purposes of easier local administration, the provinces to the north-west are under the management of a Lieutenant-Governor; and in like manner the affairs of the Punjaub, or country of the five rivers, are under the direction of a separate board of officers.

But although the whole of India is thus amenable to British sway, it must not be supposed that the revenues of the country are monopolized by us. There are large tracts entirely under the government of native princes, who merely pay *kist*, or tribute, to the English, and others to which, for a slight consideration, we extend the mantle of protection. To make each division and the actual extent of our authority more clear and obvious, it will be advisable to show in detail how the territory is allotted.

The Bengal Presidency is separated into regulation and non-regulation divisions: in other words, into provinces which are governed entirely on our system, and subject to our laws and regulations, and provinces which, as having come under our rule since the revenue system was established, are managed, in some degree, according to their ancient usage.

The Bengal regulation districts, or *collectorates*, as they are called, are seven in number—all in the lower or eastern part of India: viz., Jessore, Bhaugulpore, Cuttack, Moorshedabad, Dacca, Patna, and Chittagong. These embrace 113,702 square miles, and a population of 36,848,981.

The non-regulation provinces are Saugor and Nerbudda, Cis-Sutlej, North-eastern Frontier, Galpara, Tenasserim, South-west Frontier, the Punjaub, and the Sunderbunds, enclosed in an area of 211,950 square miles, and having a population of 11,109,339 persons.

The regulation provinces subject to the jurisdiction of the Lieut.-Governor of the North-western Provinces, whose head-quarters are at the city of Agra, are Delhi, Meerut, Rohilcund, Agra, Allahabad, and Benares, covering 71,972 square miles, and containing 23,200,000 human beings. The non-regulation provinces are of small extent. They consist of the Bhattie territory, Kumaon, Ajmere, &c., comprehended in 13,599 square miles, and having 600,000 inhabitants.

The Madras Presidency is divided for revenue purposes into twenty-one collectorates, eighteen of which are under the regulations of the Madras government; viz., Rajahmundry, Masulipatam, Guntoor, Nellore, Chingleput, Madras, Arcot (south and north), Bellary, Cuddapah, Salem, Coimbatore, Trichinopoly, Tanjore, Madura, Tinnevelly, Malabar, and Canara. These are regulation districts. The provinces of Ganjam, Vizagapatam, and Kurnaul, are non-regulation, under the control of the agents of the Governor.

All these districts cover 144,889 square miles, and contain a population of 16,339,426.

The Bombay Presidency is divided into thirteen collectorates, and three non-regulation provinces. The collectorates are Surat, Broach, Ahmedabad, Kaira, Candeish, Tannah, Poonah, Ahmednuggur, Sholapore, Belgaum, Darwar, Rutnagherry, and the island of Bombay. The non-regulation provinces are Colaba, Scinde, and Sattara. The whole of these collectorates and provinces are embraced in an area of 120,065 square miles, and the population amounts to 10,485,000 persons.

The Native states which are immediately controlled by the East India Company, because they lie within the limits of its political supremacy, without being under its direct rule, are as follows:—

The *Nizam's Territory* in the Deccan, whereof the capital is Hyderabad.

The *Kingdom of Oude*, the capital of which is Lucknow.

The *Kingdom of Nepaul*, the chief town of which is Khatmandoo.

The *Rajahship of Berar*—capital, Nagpore.

The *Dominions of Scindia*, including Bundlecund, the Saugor and Nerbudda territories, Gwalior, and a multitude of small states.

*Indore*, the capital of which is Indore.

The *Bhopal States*.—The states of Rajpootana.—Rampore.

The *Hill States*—Certain small states contiguous to Delhi.—The *Cis-Sutlej States*—Numerous small states on the south-west frontier.—*Bhawulpore*, on the left bank of the Sutlej.—Several petty and hill states on the north-eastern frontier.—*Cochin*.—The *Guicowar's dominions*, of which Baroda is the seat of Government.—The Chieftainship of *Kattiwar*.—The states of Pahlunpore, Cambay, and Ballasinore, near the collectorate of Kaira.—Darampore, Baroda, and Sucheen, contiguous to the British agency of Surat.—The Daung Rajahs, near the Ahmednuggur collectorate.—*Kolapore.*—*Sawant Warree.*—*Myhee Caunta.*—*Cutch.* Certain Sattarah Jaghiredars, and the Jaghiredars of the Southern Mahratta country.

All these *quasi* independent states cover an area of 690,360 square miles, and boast a population of 52,400,000 persons. They are controlled, advised with or watched over, by British political residents, agents to the Governor-General, commissioners, political superintendents, or revenue collectors.

It has been mentioned above that the Government of India is entrusted to the Governor-General, two Governors, a Lieut.-Governor, and Commissioners.

The Governor-General is assisted by a Supreme Council, consisting of two civil members, one military member, and one extraordinary member, who is entrusted with the preparation of acts and laws. The Commander-in-Chief of the Army is likewise a member of the Council *ex officio.*

The Governors of the minor Presidencies, have each the assistance of a Council consisting of two civil and one military member, the latter being the Commander-in-Chief of the Army of the Presidency.

The whole of the civil administration of the country is in the hands of a few hundred gentlemen who, having received their education at the college of Haileybury, Hertfordshire, obtain their appointments from the East India Directors. Their qualifications for office amount to an acquaintance with one or more of the native languages, a smattering of law and moral philosophy, and the ordinary accomplishments of gentlemen. In their hands are all the judicial, fiscal, and political offices. They commence their career on a salary of 300 rupees (30*l.*) per mensem, and rise by gradation, in the course of fifteen or twenty years, to the receipt of 5,000*l.* to 10,000*l.* per annum. The moral responsibility of these functionaries is great, and their labours, in some offices, enormous; seeing that, in many cases, a single civilian exercises control over a district 4,000 square miles in extent, and inhabited by a mixed population of 50,000 souls.

In the several towns of Calcutta, Madras, and Bombay, and in the settlements on the Malayan Peninsula, are courts of law, presided over by judges who have been trained at Westminster Hall, and who administer justice on the principles and after the forms of the Court of Queen's Bench, Common Pleas, Exchequer, and so forth. The practitioners in these courts are men who have gone through the ordinary course of preparation in the inns of court in London, and the suitors enjoy all the advantages attending litigation in England, not excluding its expenses and its glorious uncertainty. The judges in these Supreme and Recorder's Courts receive their appointments from the Board of Commissioners for the Affairs of India, and are quite independent of the Company's Governors.

The ecclesiastical establishment in India is upon a liberal and a wholesome footing. Each Presidency forms a separate diocese; the clergy are stipendiary, drawing their salaries from the East India Company. On their first appointment they receive 600*l.* a year, as assistant chaplains, and, as vacancies occur, they rise to the rank of senior chaplains, of whom there are two or three classes; the highest exercising their functions at the chief towns, and deriving, in addition to salaries of 1,200*l.* to 1,500*l.* per annum, all the advantages accruing from marriage, baptismal, and burial fees.

In addition to the clergy of the Establishment, there are ministers of the Presbyterian Church (likewise salaried from the revenues of India), Roman Catholic bishops and priests, and a great number of Church and

Baptist ministers, whose chief mission is the propagation of gospel truth, and the conversion of the Hindoos. Many of these worthy men have distinguished themselves by their learning, their piety, and zeal; and if their success in the work of proselytism has not kept pace with their exertions, it should be remembered that in no part of the world do ignorance and superstition do such stout battle for the perpetuation of idolatry and the rejection of Christianity.

It has often been maintained that our rule in India is only upheld by the sword. The allegation is but partially true. Compare the extent of the force with the gross population, and it at once becomes evident that in the moral weight of Great Britain lies the grand secret of her dominance. There are 150 milllions of natives of India, and the military force employed to hold them in subjection, and guard the frontier, does not exceed 250,000 effective soldiers. Of what avail were one soldier to six hundred determined men? Once lose the influence resulting from the impression entertained—however erroneous or exaggerated—of our truth and sense of justice, and we lose the country altogether. As the Duke of Wellington well said, when he was governor of Seringapatam, everything should be sacrificed in order to preserve our credit for scrupulous good faith.

The enduring force of this axiom is demonstrated in the fact of the numerical strength of the Indian Army having never exceeded a quarter of a million, and of that comparatively small body all but 20,000 are natives of the country, who have taken service less from the suggestions of a warlike spirit than a conviction that their devotion would be well rewarded in the amount and regularity of pay to the effective soldier, and the pension to the invalid or wounded sepoy.

Each Presidency has an army, separately commanded and separately recruited. The organization of each is, however, the same. There are European troops, forming a part of the royal army of Great Britain; European regiments of infantry, recruited expressly for the East India Company; native regulars, and native irregulars.

The Bengal Army consists of—

Three brigades of horse artillery, composed of Europeans and natives.

Six battalions of European foot artillery.

Three battalions of native ditto.

An engineer corps.

Eleven regiments of light cavalry.

Two regiments of European fusiliers.

Seventy-four regiments of sepoys.

Thirty-one irregular regiments, so called because they are officered from the regular army, but have a lesser complement of officers, and are differently paid and costumed; a corps of Guides; eighteen local corps, of varied strength, each raised for service in a particular district (chiefly in the hills); and contingent irregular corps in certain native states.

In addition to this army, are twelve regiments of Her Majesty's service, two of which are light dragoons, for which the East India Company pay.

The Bengal Army is commanded by a general officer of Her Majesty's service, who is, at the same time, Commander-in-Chief *in India.* He does not interfere in the general control of the armies of the other Presidencies; but, representing the sovereign, to him alone is confided the review of the courts-martial held on Queen's officers, and the confirmation of the sentence; and the promotion and appointment of Queen's officers to fill vacancies, pending the receipt of a decision from the Horse Guards. In the performance of these duties the Commander-in-Chief in India is assisted by a deputy adjutant and a deputy quarter-master general of

Queen's troops, several general officers, each of whom commands a division, and a numerous staff.

The Madras Army—likewise commanded by a lieutenant-general of the royal service—consists of—

One brigade of horse artillery, composed of four European and two native troops.

Four battalions of European, and one of native, foot artillery.

A corps of engineers.

Eight regiments of light cavalry.

A regiment of European fusiliers.

A regiment of European light infantry.

Fifty-two regiments of native infantry.

In addition to these are five regiments of European infantry, and one of light dragoons, or hussars, of the royal service.

Two or three general officers (one of whom belongs to the royal army) command the divisions of the army, and the staff is selected from the officers of the line.

The Bombay Army is smaller than either of the others, because the territory subject to the Bombay government is of much lesser extent. It is composed of—

One brigade of horse artillery.

Two battalions of European foot artillery.

Two battalions of native ditto.

A corps of engineers.

Three regiments of light cavalry.

One regiment of European fusiliers.

One regiment of European light infantry.

Twenty-nine regiments of native infantry, and fourteen or fifteen irregular regiments of varied strength and composition.

Three regiments of British infantry, and one of hussars, are lent by the Queen, and paid for by the Company.

The annual expense of these combined armies aver-ages ten millions sterling, arising from the necessarily liberal character of the pay and allowances. An ensign — the lowest commissioned grade — receives from 18*l.* to 20*l.* per mensem; a general officer on the staff draws 4,000*l.* per annum; and the salaries of the Commanders-in-Chief range from 8,000*l.* to 14,000*l.* per annum.

All the staff offices, and many appointments which elsewhere are filled by civilians, are in India held by military men, and the salaries are upon a very generous scale. Amongst those appointments which in the British army are held by civilians, but which in India are open to the ambition of officers, may bé mentioned the offices connected with the administration of military law, called judge-advocates and deputy judge-advocates; the army and the ordnance commissariat; the surveyorships; the superintendence of the police of the interior; the audit department; political residencies and assistantships; educational offices, &c. &c.

The medical department of the India armies consists of surgeons and assistant-surgeons. There are one or more of these officers attached to each regiment, assisted by natives, who have been duly educated in the healing art; and the remainder are scattered over the country in special charge of hospitals, gaols, colleges, and the civil community of a station, or district. The medical department is controlled by medical boards and superintending surgeons, who are the oldest and most experienced persons in the service. These latter appointments are well remunerated, and fall to the surgeons in virtue of seniority and superior skill. Medical officers are permitted to practise their profession among persons who are not in the Company's service, and this—a very large source of profit—makes an appointment to one of the chief towns of the Presidencies an object of great ambition.

The appointments to the India service, both civil

and military, are vested in the members of the Court of East India Directors. Each director has a certain number of writerships (as nominations to the civil department are called), and cadetships, or military commissions. All writers proceed at once to the college at Haileybury, and must remain there four terms, drinking in such knowledge as is supposed to fit them for the offices they are destined to fill. No writer must be under seventeen years of age when he enters the college, nor more than twenty-three when he quits its walls to proceed to India. Cadets, if intended for the artillery or engineers, are required to proceed to Addiscombe College. Their stay here is limited to four terms, but they may pass through the seminary as rapidly as their attainments and qualifications will enable them to pass, after a year's residence, provided that they are of the age of sixteen before the day of their final examination. If they do not, after the four terms, get through the examination required for the artillery and engineers, they are appointed to the cavalry and infantry. *Direct,* or infantry and cavalry, cadetships do not involve the necessity for a residence at the college. It is only requisite that the young men should be examined in history, geography, fortification, Latin, French (or Hindostanee), mathematics, and writing from dictation. If they have received the education of gentlemen they are considered fit for cadets.

Assistant-surgeoncies are in like manner in the gift of individual Directors. The candidate must pass an examination in surgery by the Royal College of Surgeons, unless he possesses a diploma from the Royal College of Surgeons, or the colleges of Dublin, Edinburgh, or Glasgow. He must also pass an examination by the East India Company's examining physician in the practice of physic.

The seas of India enjoy protection from a fleet of

British men-of-war, and of steamers and small frigates and sloops belonging to the East India Company. The latter are officered by persons appointed midshipmen, in the first instance, by the Directors. They must not be under fifteen nor above eighteen years of age, when first sent out, unless they shall have served on board a steam-vessel, or under an engineer in a factory or foundry. In India they serve either on board the steam-packets which ply between Bombay and Aden, or in the schooners and small frigates employed in the Persian Gulf, China, and the Straits of Malacca; and in the surveys of the seas and coasts in the East. Midshipmen rise to the rank of lieutenants, commanders, and captains. There is no higher rank in the service than captain. The Indian navy is commanded, or superintended, by a captain of the British navy.

Liberal as is the scale of remuneration to all classes of persons serving the East India Company, it is in the arrangements made for securing a provision to those who may have devoted their years and energies to that Company that the advantage of belonging to the service is most apparent. It is true that the obligation of contributing to his own future support and that of his brethren, their widows, orphans, and families, is compulsory upon the officer; but it is quite certain that without the countenance and generous support of the East India Company, none of the provisions made for the "rainy day" could hold.

To improve the health and repair the constitutions of those who may suffer from a prolonged residence in the East, furloughs are allowed to all ranks of the service; and during such absence from their duties, a certain amount of pay is granted, and the various Civil, Military, and Medical Funds contribute sums proportionate to the rank and services of the individual. Thus, a civilian on furlough to Europe draws 500*l.* a year; military officers receive the net pay of their rank, and their respective Funds grant them additions, varying from 50*l.* to 150*l.* per annum, if they stand in need of such assistance. Hitherto, military men have only been allowed one furlough of three years' duration in the course of their service, and this rule was framed many years ago, when voyages were of six months' duration, and the opportunities of going to and fro very rare. But efforts are now making to procure an alteration, dictated by the modern facilities of effecting a visit to England, and the advantage of enabling gentlemen to pay more than one visit to Europe in the course of thirty years, and there can be little doubt that these efforts will be attended with success.

Upon their ultimate retirement from the Company's service, civilians, if they have regularly subscribed to their Funds, receive annuities of 500*l.* or 1,000*l.* per annum, according to their length of service. The regulations for the retirement of the military and other officers are as follow:—

Officers who have served less than three years in India, and have lost their health there, are entitled to an allowance from Lord Clive's Fund, if the Court of Directors shall adjudge them to be proper objects of that bounty, to the extent of—If a second lieutenant, cornet, or ensign, 2*s.* a day, or 36*l.* 10*s.* a year; if a lieutenant, 2*s.* 6*d.* a day, or 45*l.* 12*s.* 6*d.* a year; provided they are not possessed of, or entitled to, real or personal property to the extent of, if an ensign, 750*l.*, if a lieutenant, 1,000*l.*

"Officers who are compelled to quit the service by wounds received in action, or by ill-health contracted on duty after three years' service in India, are permitted to retire on the half-pay of their rank; viz.—If a second lieutenant, cornet, or ensign, 3*s.* a day, or 54*l.* per annum; if a lieutenant, 4*s.* a day, or 73*l.* per annum.

"A subaltern officer, or assistant-surgeon, having

served six years in India, is permitted to retire on the half-pay of ensign, if his constitution should be so impaired as to prevent the possibility of his continuing in India.

"A lieutenant having served thirteen, or a second-lieutenant, cornet, or ensign, nine years in India (including three years for a furlough), may retire on the half-pay of his rank, in case his health shall not permit him to serve in India.

"Regimental captains, majors, and lieutenant-colonels, who have not served sufficiently long in India to entitle them to retire on full pay, and whose ill-health renders it impossible for them to continue to serve in India, are allowed to retire from the service on the half-pay of their ranks, viz:—

"Captains, 7*s.* a day, or 127*l.* 15*s.* per annum; major, 9*s.* 6*d.* a day, or 173*l.* 7*s.* 6*d.* per annum; lieutenant-colonel, 11*s.* a day, or 200*l.* 15*s.* per annum.

"All officers who have actually served twenty-two years in India, or twenty-five years, including three years for a furlough, are allowed to retire on the full pay of their respective ranks.

"Officers are also allowed to retire on the following pensions, without reference to the rank they may have attained, if they have served to the undermentioned periods, viz.:—

"After twenty-three years' service in India, including three years for a furlough, on the full pay of captain, viz., 191*l.* 12*s.* 6*d.* per annum; after twenty-seven years' service, including three years for a furlough, on the full pay of major, 292*l.* per annum; after thirty-one years' service in India, including three years for a furlough, on the full pay of lieutenant-colonel, 365*l.* per annum; after thirty-five years' service in India, including three years for a furlough, on the full pay of colonel, 456*l.* 5*s.* per annum.

"Members of the Medical Board, who have been in that station not less than two years, and not less than twenty years in India, including three years for one furlough, are permitted to retire from the service, and allowed 500*l.* per annum, or in the event of ill-health, they may retire on that pension, after any period of service as members of the Medical Board. If they have served *five* years, or are obliged, after three years' service in that station, to retire from ill-health, they are allowed 700*l.* per annum.

"Superintending-surgeons, who have been in that station not less than two years, and whose period of service has been not less than twenty years, including three years for one furlough, are permitted to retire from the service and allowed 300*l.* per annum; or in event of ill-health, they may retire on that pension after any period of service as superintending-surgeon. If they have served five years, or are obliged, after three years' service in that station, to retire from ill-health, they are allowed 365*l.* per annum. Surgeons after twenty years' service, three years' furlough included.......................................... £191 a-year

| | | | | | |
|---|---|---|---|---|---|
| 24 | years' service, | 3 | years' furlough | 250 | " |
| 28 | " | 3 | " | 300 | " |
| 32 | " | 3 | " | 365 | " |
| 35 | " | 3 | " | 500 | " |
| 38 | " | 3 | " | 700 | " |

"The present regulations by which superintending-surgeons are entitled as such to retiring pensions of 300*l.* and 360*l.* a year, and members of the Medical Board to pensions of 500*l.* and 700*l.* a year, according to period of service in those ranks respectively, will cease to be the rule of the service for medical officers after the date of the introduction of the new arrangement; but individuals then in the service, and who may be appointed to the offices of superintending-surgeon and member of the Board within ten years from that date, will be allowed the option of retiring upon pensions upon the old scale of length of service in those ranks instead of the new scale of length of service in India.

"When officers on furlough retire upon the pay or half-pay of their rank, they are only entitled to claim the benefits of the rank held by them at the expiration of one year from the date of their landing in the United Kingdom.

"A veterinary surgeon is allowed to retire after six years' service in India, provided his health shall not permit him to serve in India, on 4*s.* 6*d.* a day; after ten years' service in India, provided his health shall not permit him to serve in India, 5*s.* 6*d.* a day.

After 20 years' service, 3 years' furlough included .................................. 7*s.* a day.
After 25 years' service, 3 years' furlough included .................................. 8*s.* „
After 30 years' service, 3 years' furlough included .................................. 12*s.* „

"A commissary, or deputy-commissary of Ordnance, not being a commissioned officer, is allowed to retire on full pay, if he has served twenty-seven years in India, of which twelve must have been in the Ordnance department; twenty-five years, fourteen of which in that department; or twenty-two years, seventeen years of which in the Ordnance department.

"A conductor of stores is allowed to retire on 60*l.* per annum, after twenty-five years' actual service in in India.

"Officers retiring from service are considered to have retired from the date of their application for leave to retire; or from the expiration of two years and a half from their quitting India, whichever may happen first."

## CHAPTER III.

### THE ROUTES TO INDIA.

*Sea voyage—The expense—The necessary equipment—Sailing ships—Screw steamers—The overland route—The steamers of the Peninsular and Oriental Company—The cost and the equipment.*

VERY little change has taken place during the past thirty years in the voyage to India by *sailing vessels.* The same scale of entertainment, the same cabin dimensions, the same degree of speed, which distinguished the magnificent vessels of the East India Company, when that Company enjoyed a monopoly of the tea trade, now characterize the fleet belonging to the great houses of Smith, Green, and Wigram. The free traders, which, in the days when the leviathans of the Company majestically ploughed the seas, modestly confined themselves to 700 tons, have now swollen to the dimensions of the famous old East Indiamen, and the passenger by the *Marlborough,* the *Hardwicke,* &c., may fancy himself on board the *Marquis of Camden,* the *Charles Grant,* or the *Lowther Castle,* with the advantage of not finding in his cabin one of the formidable 32-pounders with which Captain Dance fought the French squadron.

The charge for a cabin in one of the crack sailing vessels is as follows. The average is given—a difference being occasionally made to suit particular circumstances:—

For the largest stern-cabins, for a family of three, 250*l*.

For the largest stern-cabins, for one person, 160*l*.

For the smaller cabins, for one person, 70*l*. to 100*l*.

The outfit necessary for a voyage is by no means so great as is alleged by those who make a livelihood (if not fortunes), by the excessive supply; but it will be difficult for any one who desires ordinary comfort and cleanliness to manage with a smaller wardrobe than the following. Allowing for the actual possession of a fair quantity of linen, cloth coats, waistcoats, and trousers, it will still be necessary that a gentleman should have—

Four dozen cotton shirts.

A dozen and a half India gauze flannel waistcoats.

Two or three dozen thin cotton socks or stockings.

Two dozen pairs of calico drawers.

Three dozen pocket-handkerchiefs; half-a-dozen neck ditto.

A couple of cotton dressing-gowns, and loose cotton trousers to correspond.

Two or three tunics of brown holland or gray alpaca.

Two or three blue or black silk, jean, or crape jackets.

Three or four dozen pairs of cotton or linen trousers.

Two dozen white cotton jackets.

Two or three alpaca, and a dozen white waistcoats.

In addition to these, the passenger will need a clothes-bag, a couch or cot, eight pairs of sheets, eight pillow-cases, two blankets and two quilts, two dozen towels; a washhand-stand, &c., a chest of drawers, a looking-glass, chair (to fold up), a cabin-lamp, tin can, soap, candles; writing-case, dressing-case, &c.; one or two large sponges will also be of great use.

Ladies proceeding to India by sea will require, besides the last-named articles for cabin use, the subjoined equipment:—

A black silk dress.
Four coloured, and four white muslin dresses.
Forty-eight calico or cambric chemises.
Twenty-four calico night-gowns.
Twenty-four night-caps.
Twelve cambric slips.
Thirty-six petticoats.
Four flannel petticoats.
Eighteen India gauze waistcoats.
Thirty-six pairs of cambric trousers.
Eight dressing-gowns.
Six dozen cambric pocket-handkerchiefs.
Four dozen towels.
Thirty-six white cotton or thread stockings.
Twelve kid gloves.

As there is seldom a library on board ship, a few books will be valuable accompaniments, and it will not be amiss if the following form part of the stock of a person intended for a residence in India: "The Oriental Interpreter and Treasury of Indian Knowledge," published by Cox and Co., King William-street, Strand; Miss Emma Roberts' "Sketches of Hindostan;" MacFarlane's "History of British India;" and Forbes' "Hindustanee Grammar and Dictionary," supposing the passenger is inclined to study the Hindostanee language.

The first attempts made thirty years ago to establish a communication between England and India round the Cape of Good Hope, were failures, in respect to an abridgment of the time consumed in a voyage. The long intervals between the coaling stations, and the period consumed in an irregular course in order to reach them, neutralized all the advantages gained by accelerated movement when under steam. Mr. Waghorn, who followed Capt. J. H. Johnston in advocating the Cape route, abandoned it in 1830, in favour of the Red Sea line. But within the last three or four years the great difficulty has been surmounted through the energy and enterprise of the General Screw Steam Shipping Company, and coaling depôts have been established upon the highway, which render the voyage easy and rapid.

On the 13th of each month, one of the large screw steamers (six of which are of 1,800 tons burthen each), leaves Southampton for Calcutta. Calling for mails at Plymouth on the 15th, the vessel proceeds to St. Vincent (Cape de Verds), thence to Ascension, the Cape of Good Hope, Mauritius, and so up to Point de Galle, Ceylon, Madras, and Calcutta, which place is generally reached in sixty days from the date of departure from Southampton. The accommodation on board these vessels is divided into three classes: First-class cabins for ladies and families; secondly, family cabins in the fore part of the ship; and, thirdly, general cabins. Writers, cadets, and "other young gentlemen" proceeding to Calcutta for the first time, pay 80*l.* each in a general cabin; to Madras they pay 75*l.*; and to Ceylon, 70*l.* Other persons pay as follows:—

| | To Ceylon. | To Madras. | To Calcutta. |
|---|---|---|---|
| One person . . . . . . . . . . | £81 | £82 10 | £90 |
| Do. occupying a double cabin . | 101 | 102 0 | 115 |
| Two persons, occupying a treble cabin | 192 | 205 0 | 220 |

By "one person" is meant an individual who merely occupies a berth in a cabin which contains two or three other berths. The other charges arise out of the entire appropriation of a cabin by one or two persons.

There are cabins, with certain private accommodations attached to them, which bear a still higher price.

The sums paid, as above, comprehend the advantages of an excellent table, exclusive of wines, beer, and spirituous liquors, which are charged for separately—a good and equitable arrangement, for very many persons do not consume either one or the other, or at least in a very moderate quantity, and it is hardly reasonable to expect them to pay for what they do not consume.

The charges for children above two years of age (all below that age without a berth, and with their parents, are free) are:—

| With the Parents:— | To Ceylon. | To Madras. | To Calcutta. |
|---|---|---|---|
| 5 years and under 10 . . . | £40 | £42 0 | £45 |
| 2 years and under 5 . . . | 27 | 28 10 | 36 |
| Servants—European . . . . | 30 | 32 0 | 36 |
| " Native . . . . . | 23 | 25 0 | 28 |

Each adult passenger pays a fee of 2*l.* to the steward of the vessel, and for each child, a fee of 1*l.* is payable.

Passengers are expected to embark at Southampton, shipping their baggage two clear days before the time appointed for the departure of the ship. Each grown person is allowed thirty cubic feet of baggage; children and servants half that quantity. After the shipment of the baggage, nothing is allowed to be taken on board but a portmanteau, carpet-bag, and hat-box. No trunks, boxes, or portmanteaus, are allowed in the cabins.

The office of the General Screw Steam Shipping Company is at No. 2, Royal Exchange-buildings, City. On application to the secretary the fullest particulars are obtainable.

The equipment required by a gentleman or lady proceeding by this route will be a medium between what has been suggested for a sea voyage and what is indispensably necessary for a trip overland. The time consumed is ten or twelve days more than the latter, and twenty to thirty days less than the former.

There are several ways of reaching India by land and sea combined; but for the accomplishment of that route which is popularly known as "the overland," remarkable facilities have existed during the past twelve years.

Persons who desire to visit the continent, or wish to have as little of the sea voyage as possible, will proceed through France to Marseilles, or through Germany to Trieste on the Adriatic. At either of these ports they find vessels which convey them to Alexandria.

For the conveyance of passengers and packets by the first-named route, the Peninsular and Oriental Company built and equipped a fleet of superb steamers, and it is by one of these a person anxious to make the best of his way to India, will undoubtedly proceed.

The Peninsular and Oriental Company's steamers leave Southampton on the 4th and 20th of every month, at one o'clock P.M., excepting when the appointed day of departure falls upon a Sunday, when the sailing of the vessel is postponed to one o'clock P.M. on the following day. In five days the steamer reaches Gibraltar, the rock famous in modern history as the scene of a gallant exploit in the reign of Queen Anne (when the place fell into our possession), and a noble defence in the reign of George the Third, when for between three and four years the wise and brave Sir Gilbert Elliott, afterwards Lord Heathfield, held out against the combined fleets and arms of Spain and France. Twelve hours' delay, while the steamer takes in coal, affords an opportunity to the passenger of landing, and taking a survey of the town—a curious *mélange* of architecture and horticulture — and the vessel then proceeds on her course, reaching Malta in five days more. Here a delay of twenty-four hours presents an occasion for a ramble through the principal streets, a visit to the churches and albergas, and a short drive beyond the walls of the town. Four days after quitting Malta, the steamer arrives at Alexandria. Here the passengers are landed with their baggage, and embarking in small steamers, at once proceed up the Mahmoodie Canal — that celebrated monument of the Pacha Mahomed Ali's enterprise and cruelty — to Atfeh, where they are transhipped to other vessels, which bear them up the Nile to Cairo. Here a night's rest is obtained, while the baggage is carried across the desert to Suez, which place the passengers reach by carriages, by the evening of the following day. The entire journey from Alexandria to Suez thus divided, occupies about sixty hours, allowing, besides the night's rest, ample time for refreshment and repose at the central station or hotel between Cairo and Suez.

In six days from the time of reaching Suez, where the traveller embarks on a steamer corresponding in all respects with the splendid vessel he has quitted at Alexandria, he arrives at Aden, a military and coaling depôt at the south-easterly extremity of the Straits of Babelmandeb. Twenty-four hours suffice for the reception of coal, and then the Indian Ocean is crossed. On the thirty-fourth day from the date of departure from Southampton, the island of Ceylon is reached. In five days more the steamer gets to Madras, and three days later she casts anchor in the river Hooghly, opposite the splendid city of Calcutta. The whole voyage is thus accomplished in about sixty days.

Supposing a person determines to take the "overland route" to India, he books himself for a passage at the office of the Peninsular and Oriental Company, No. 122, Leadenhall-street, City. The rates of passage-money are as follow; and, unlike those of the General Screw Steam Shipping Company, include table, wines, stewards' fees, &c., for first-class passengers. The expense of transit through Egypt is also comprehended in the scale, with the exception of hotel expenses, and of *extra* baggage, wines, beer, spirits, and soda water, all of which the Egyptian transit administration charge for separately.

| | Ceylon. | Madras. | Calcutta, or Penang. | Singapore. |
|---|---|---|---|---|
| *Gentlemen*, travelling singly, occupying a berth in a Cabin, with two or three others on the *Lower* Deck; and *Ladies*, travelling singly, occupying a berth in a Cabin, with two or three others on the *Upper* Deck | £95 | £100 | £105 | £110 |
| *Married Couples*, occupying a reserved Cabin on the Main Deck . . . . | 240 | 250 | 270 | 290 |
| *Children*, with their Parents, 3 years and under 10 . | 48 | 50 | 53 | 55 |
| A Child under 3 years of age, *free*. | | | | |
| Servants—European . . | 43 | 46 | 50 | 52 |
| " Native . . . | 26 | 28 | 30 | 31 |

At Aden the passengers intending to proceed to Bombay are transferred to a steamer belonging to the East India Company, and conveyed to Bombay for 30*l*. a head. The passage from Southampton to Aden in the Peninsular and Oriental Company's steamer costs 70*l*.

In the steamers of the Peninsular and Oriental Company, first-class passengers are allowed three hundredweight of personal baggage free of freight. Children and servants are allowed 1½ cwt. each.

But a person taking a whole cabin is permitted to have one-half more baggage than the regulated allowance. The Egyptian Transit Company, however, demand 14*s*. per cwt. for conveyance of baggage through, should it exceed 2 cwt. for first-class passengers, and 1 cwt. each for servants and children. No package of baggage must exceed 80 lbs. weight, or measure more than 3 ft. in length—1 ft. 3 in. in breadth—and 1 ft. 2 in. in depth. A departure from this regulation causes a detention in Egypt to such packages of a fortnight.

As soon as the baggage is embarked it is placed below in the baggage room, no passenger being allowed to take trunks, boxes, or portmanteaus, in the saloon or cabin; but on application to the captain the baggage can be had up during the passage.

It is of importance that every package should bear the name of the owner in legible characters, and that the passage-money be paid before the passenger attempt to embark.

The *minimum* equipment requisite for the overland trip is as follows. Gentlemen and ladies can increase this quantity *ad libitum,* but it should be remembered that a portion of the articles with which they may supply themselves are not needed in India, and will only prove an encumbrance when the voyage is at an end. We make no distinction in the supplies required by writers and cadets, for it is presumed that all gentlemen like to make the same appearance. Discarding, then, the soft persuasions of the wily outfitter, and remembering that the cheap and the good are not always synonymous, let the intending traveller, when he has engaged his passage, hie to Killick, 7, Ludgate Hill, or Thresher and Glenny, Strand, and equip himself with—

Four dozen cotton shirts; three dozen pairs of cotton socks or stockings; a dozen India gauze flannel waistcoats; two dozen pairs of calico drawers; three dozen silk pocket handkerchiefs; half a dozen silk cravats, black and coloured; two or three pairs of loose printed cotton trousers (for bathing purposes); a couple of cotton dressing gowns; a cashmere or merino jacket; a couple of Alpaca (gray) tunics or blouzes; two or three dozen pairs of white trousers; a dozen cotton or jean waistcoats; a straw hat with broad brim; a cloth cap; a dressing-case; a writing-case (well filled); a large bag for foul linen; and a couple of good large leather trunks to contain the whole stock. It is concluded that every one possesses a sufficiency of cloth coats, trousers, hats, gloves, boots and shoes. At all events a very small supply is requisite, for a few days after quitting the shores of England tropical clothing is indispensable, and continues so to the end of the voyage. No towels or sheets are necessary, for these are all provided in the steamer.

A lady will require for the trip about one-half the articles recommended for the sea voyage in a previous page.

# CHAPTER IV.

## THE EMIGRANT TO INDIA.

*The European population of India—Its character and extent—Advice to emigrants—Equipment for such persons.*

INDIA, though the largest, richest, and most valuable appendage to the British crown, offers the smallest inducement to the general emigrant of any of the foreign dominions of the sovereign. The nature of the climate effectually closing the door against the common labourer, and the low rate of wages for which the most ingenious native artisans can afford to work, putting competition on the part of the English mechanic quite out of the question, the only classes who can expect to make way in India are those who have a sufficiency of capital to purchase plantations, or start in business on their own account, or are sufficient masters of an art of which the natives are ignorant to be acceptable as foremen in large establishments. These persons, and the various employés of the Government, constitute the European population of British India—a wonderfully small population compared with the millions of aborigines, yet a highly prosperous and intelligent body, to whose energy and moral conduct the ruling country owes, in a great measure, the secret of her power.

To speak more definitely and distinctly, the European community of British India consists of the civil and military officers of the East India Company, the European troops belonging to the royal army, bishops and judges, clergymen, barristers and attorneys, merchant-seamen (captains and mates of ships), merchants, shopkeepers, medical practitioners, indigo and sugar planters, missionaries, clerks, artists, musicians, printers, livery-stable keepers, &c.; in all some fifty thousand individuals, of whom twenty thousand are European soldiers.

Until within the last twenty years it was a high crime and misdemeanour for any European to be in India without an appointment, or a special license from the Directors of the East India Company. Every person who was not in the service of the government could only proceed to India with the indentures of a "free merchant," or a "free mariner," both of which were obtained at the India House with some difficulty, under recognizances and securities that the applicant was a person of good character, and seriously meant either to carry on business as a merchant, or to become a mate or commander of a country vessel. Now and then some highly favoured individuals procured permission to "reside" in India, but they were always watched with jealous anxiety by the Government, lest they should employ their privilege to poison the native mind, bring the authorities into disrepute, and set society by the ears. When the East India Company were deprived of their commercial privileges in 1833, and the act was passed which limited them to territorial control and the exercise of political functions in relation to India and the states immediately contiguous to the empire, all this jealous exclusion of "interlopers" came to an end, and the door was opened to the free ingress of persons who chose to make India the scene of their exertions. The result has been advantageous to the country in the more general diffusion of European intelligence, especially as practical and legal freedom has been given to the press, and the natives have received in a large degree the advantages of education; and something has been done to evolve the agricultural resources of India by the application of European capital and energy to the cultivation of the soil. But, on the whole, the removal of restraints upon the resort of Englishmen to India has not been attended by all the results contemplated by the advocates of the abolition of the trading charter, nor, at the same time, have any of the fears of the enemies of colonization been realized. A wide field still exists for the profitable employment of industry, intelligence, and capital, and there can be little doubt that when railways have been established, and practicable roads formed to facilitate communication with the fertile districts of upper and central India, a greater number of Europeans will find their way to the country.

The best advice which, under present circumstances, can be given to persons desirous of emigrating to India, for the purpose of obtaining an independent existence, or of improving their means, is, that they should carry with them letters of introduction to men in authority, or a sufficiency of capital to obtain shares in, if not exclusive possession of, indigo, sugar, or coffee plantations, saltpetre manufactories, &c. Through the letters of introduction, if sustained by a fair share of talent and a good address, a young man may obtain employment as a clerk, superintendent, deputy collector or magistrate, assistant to a planter, sub-editor of a newspaper, reporter, mate or master of a river steamer, and so on — offices which yield generally from one hundred to five hundred rupees per mensem. But these offices are not numerous, are competed for by intelligent natives and East Indians, and are not recognized, when obtained, as bringing the holder within the pale of good society. If a young man has had the advantage of a legal education in England, or happens to be connected with any of the lawyers who are appointed judges of the several Supreme Courts, he may, perhaps, become a clerk to one of the "reverend signors," or a sealer, or procure leave to practise as an attorney (after due qualification); and there are occasional openings for young medical practitioners who are not above contenting themselves with such fees as the parsimony of the natives may induce them to offer—but all these must be regarded as prizes in a lottery, in which the blanks are numerous, and every adventurer must be prepared to support himself for some time, if he has not hospitable friends and relatives at one of the presidencies, who will give him house and home until a situation of some sort is available.

The young man who arrives in India with a small capital, and a capacity to be useful, is in a much more hopeful condition than he who merely carries with him thews, sinews, brains, introductions, and an engaging deportment. There are always brokers, agents, planters, small merchants, auctioneers, newspaper proprietors, ship-builders, boat-builders, and tradesmen enough in every town, disposed to extend their sphere of operations by accepting as a partner one who can bring a little money and considerable intelligence and personal activity to the common stock. Many a youth proceeding to India, thus prepared, has, ere now, risen to a state of affluence in a comparatively short time; and—for the truth must be told—not a few have experienced the vicissitudes incidental to commerce and speculation.

Addressing ourselves to these classes of intending adventurers to India, we should say, "Content yourselves with a moderate equipment; arm yourselves with patience, which is ever the best attendant upon hope, resolve when in India to practise temperance, and the chances are greatly in favour of your doing well, and of retiring to your native country with an unbroken constitution."

We have spoken of a "moderate equipment." This brings us to the details of outfit, and we fear that we shall be deemed guilty of heresy in counselling a wide departure from the advice generally given on this head, especially by those who find their account in overloading the passenger. Of course there is a great difference in the quantity of articles required for a sea voyage, and those needed for an overland trip, because the one is twice the duration of the other; but in no case is it necessary for a young man to burthen himself to the extent recommended by professional outfitters.

The following scale may be confidently offered as suited to either route—the sea or overland.

### Overland.

One dozen pair of cotton stockings.
Ditto cotton socks.
Three dozen shirts.
One dozen of India gauze waistcoats.
Ditto calico drawers.
Two dozen silk pocket handkerchiefs.
Two black silk cravats.
Two pairs of braces.
One cotton dressing-gown.
One pair of pyjamas.
One clothes bag.
One straw hat (with veil for crossing the desert.)

One cloth cap.
One cashmere or merino jacket.
Twelve pairs of white cotton trousers.
Six pairs of Holland trousers.
Twelve white or printed cotton or jean waistcoats.
Two Holland or Alpaca blouses.
A dozen towels.
A large sponge.
A leathern writing-case.
Overland trunks and a carpet-bag.

N.B.—It is presumed that a hat, a dress coat, frock, trousers, boots, shoes, slippers, brushes, neckerchiefs, are already in the traveller's possession.

## By Sea.

Two dozen pairs of cotton stockings.
One dozen ditto of cotton socks.
Four dozen day shirts.
Two dozen night ditto.
One and a half dozen of gauze waistcoats.
Three dozen silk pocket handkerchiefs.
Three black silk cravats.
Three pairs of braces.
Two cotton dressing-gowns and a couple of pair of pyjanas or loose cotton trousers.
A straw hat and a cloth cap.
A couple of Merino or camlet jackets.
A couple of Alpaca or Holland blouses or tunics.
Twelve white and twelve coloured waistcoats.
Eighteen pairs of white cotton or linen trousers.
One dozen pairs of check cashmerette ditto.
Three dozen towels.
One dozen pairs of sheets and pillow-cases, with blankets and a quilt.

A cot or hammock—the former preferable because of permanent utility.

A wash-hand stand and appurtenances.

A clothes-bag; piece of carpeting or floor-cloth for cabin; a foot-tub; a chest of drawers; a looking-glass; camp chair; cabin lamp; tin can; and a few books.

In respect to coats, waistcoats, and trousers, the passenger will suit himself. It should be remembered that, for the first ten days of the voyage, and for the fortnight during which the vessel is rounding the Cape, the weather is sufficiently cold to render woollen clothes particularly acceptable.

# CHAPTER V.

## EUROPEAN LIFE IN INDIA.

*European life in India—The kind of houses required—Method of furnishing—Domestics—Articles of life—Markets—Household expenses—Amusements and resources—Diet—Routine of existence—Literature—Life in the Mofussil—The indigo planter—Life of a lady in India—Children.*

How to live, where to live, and what to live upon, are questions which agitate all classes of Englishmen who are not born with silver spoons in their mouths—in other words, who are not born independent of the world's cares. To be able to make both ends meet is the anxious consideration of four-fifths of the British population; but those who betake themselves to India and the colonies carry their solicitude beyond that point—they wish to know not merely if their incomes will support them in comfort, but if they will leave a margin sufficiently broad to afford a fund for a provision in old age. In his native land a man is content with a moderate sum; for to the means of existence he adds the inestimable advantage of living in a mild climate among friends and relatives he has learned to value, and by whom he is esteemed. In India, on the other hand, he does battle with a noxious climate, and is separated from those he loves best. It therefore becomes a consideration whether expatriation is to be attended with the advantage of a return to England with a competency; for, otherwise, it would be better to remain at home on bread and cheese. In the case of persons going out with appointments in the East India Company's service, the question, as we have shown, is placed beyond a doubt; for the enforced subscriptions to civil and military funds, and the conditions of the pension establishment, relieve a man of all care for the remote future, if he never desires to grow rich by his savings. It is far otherwise with the adventurer who has nothing definite to calculate upon. He knows that his only hope of doing well depends upon a well regulated economy, and he shapes his course accordingly.

The system of lodging-letting so common in England and the continent is almost unknown in India. Something is done in the boarding-house way at the chief towns by respectable widows, and each presidency is provided with respectable hotels and club-houses; but no one seeks or desires a permanent residence at any of these places. They afford excellent temporary accommodation to persons newly arrived in India, and upon a scale adapted to all sorts of purses; but when the stranger has had time to look about him, he quits them for a more frugal and enduring style of life. The writer goes to his station, the cadet or assistant-surgeon to his regiment, and the resident, who is neither civil nor military, seeks a house suited to his means, or to the appearance he must necessarily keep up. Let him not expect to find a furnished house anywhere—such things are unknown in India; for when the occupants of mansions quit the presidency for the interior they take everything away with them; and if they return to England all the property is sold off by auction to ensure the means of settling at home. This practice, however, of selling off, causes an enormous quantity of capital second-hand furniture to be always available in the *godowns* or store-houses of the auctioneers; and if new furniture is preferred, there are scores of upholsterers' shops where articles can always be obtained at a few hours' notice. A stranger, on these occasions, after he has looked about for an empty house adapted to his wants, sends for a *sircar* (at Calcutta), a *dubash* (at Madras), or a Parsee butler (at Bombay), and bidding him procure the necessary furniture, may expect in two or three days to find himself installed in his own domicile. The articles absolutely required at first are few, as nothing in the shape of fixtures or hangings is required. Matting for two or three rooms—say a dining-room, drawing-room, and a couple of bed-rooms —or one bed-room, with bathing and dressing apartment attached. A cot with gauze curtains, a wash-hand-stand, dressing-table, towel-horse, chest of drawers,* &c., will suffice for the bed-room; a table, half a dozen chairs, a sofa, and a few book-shelves, will suffice for the drawing-room; a table, half a dozen chairs, and a small side-board, are furniture enough for a dining-room. To these add a *punkah*, or large fan upon an oblong frame, which is suspended from the ceiling of each sitting-room with a rope attached to it, that a servant may keep it continually swinging when the room is occupied. A few plates, dishes, cups and saucers, spoons, knives and forks, a table-lamp and a hanging-lamp, some water jars, and the commonest earthen cooking utensils, will complete the household equipment of a bachelor. His purchase of a horse and buggy, or a palankeen, or both, will depend upon

* The articles which have been used on board ship are often quite good and handsome enough for these purposes.

his business, his inclination, and his means. One or the other will be unavoidable, because it is impossible for any person to walk to his place of business, or to go to the houses and offices of those with whom he may have transactions. Pedestrianism, excepting for a leisure stroll early in the morning and the cool of the evening, is impossible. But if a man determines to be severely parsimonious, and has not the wherewithal to purchase a palankeen, he can hire one every day to take him to and from his shop or counting-house, or wherever else his business may lead him. A better plan still will be, for a tradesman or merchant, to take a house which will answer all the purposes of a domicile and a place of business. The lower floors of houses make capital offices and shops.

The expense of "life" at one of the Presidencies depends upon the circumstances and position of the individual. A man may live on 200*l.* a year, or 170 rupees per mensem; and he may also spend without difficulty 10,000*l.* a year. The size of the house, the number of servants, horses, and carriages, and the extensive exercise of private hospitality and public charity, make all the difference. To give an idea of the maximum of expenditure, we will suppose an establishment at Calcutta upon a grand scale.

A house of two stories, containing twenty rooms and broad verandas, with bathing-rooms and out-offices, all enclosed within a garden or compound, costs at least 500 rupees per month. The establishment of servants will run as follows:—

A *khansumah*, or butler, who markets and attends at table on great occasions. He also makes pastry and preserves, and superintends the kitchen.

Two or three *khetmutgars*, who also attend at table, clean the plate, &c.

A *valet*, of the khetmutgar class, who takes care of the linen and clothes of his master, and looks after his toilet.

A *cook* and a deputy, the latter of whom attends the *khansumah* at market, and brings home the supplies.

A *sirdar* and bearers—*sirdar* meaning chief—whose duty it is to prepare the bath, polish boots and shoes, attend to the lamps and candles, and see that the bearers are ready either to pull the punkah, or to go out with the palankeen, or waft away flies and insects during the meals, or polish the furniture.

A *musalchee*, who acts the part of a scullion, and likewise prepares the lamps.

A *bheestie*, or water carrier. He draws water from the wells or tanks, and fills the jars with the water required during the day. He sprinkles the *cuscuss tatties*, or plaited grass coverings of the doors and windows, during the hot season, and waters the garden or grass plots.

A *mihtur*, or sweeper, who does all the dirty work of the house.

A *dhobee*, or washerman. There are no washerwomen in Indo-European establishments. The *modus operandi*, amounting to the beating of linen on flat stones, is performed by a man, and his wife irons the articles.

A *durzee*, or tailor. This functionary is chiefly employed in repairing the damages effected by *dhobees*, or in making bed curtains, hemming sheets and tablecloths, darning stockings, &c. His work is abundant where there is a lady and children in the house, because the lady rarely condescends to anything useful in a large establishment.

A *durwan*, or doorkeeper. He sits at the entrance gate, sounds a gong upon the arrival of a visitor, and throws open the portals of the compound. To him also is consigned the task of uttering the white lie, which announces that the master or mistress of the house is "not at home."

An *abdar*, or "keeper of the water." To him is assigned the duty of cooling the wines, beer, and water, for dinner purposes; but the introduction of American ice into India has nearly obliterated his functions.

A *coachman*, whose title announces his duty.

*Syces*, or grooms, one to each horse, or two to three horses. They not only groom and feed the horses, but either take their places behind a carriage or run by its side, or by the side of the equestrian who may be paying visits, and require his horse to be occasionally held.

A *peon*, or chuprassy. A belted messenger, who awaits to carry letters and messages, or to accompany the coachman upon state visits.

An *ayah*, or lady's maid, a very useful personage in a family; for she relieves the lady of the labour of dressing her hair, and is most serviceable in *shampooing* and performing a number of delicate little offices which the heat of the climate often renders necessary. It is needless to add that she dresses her mistress, and looks after her wardrobe, and *dhobee's* accounts.

A *mihturanee*, or *metrannee*, a female sweeper, whose services are auxiliary to those of the *ayah*.

A *sircar*, who keeps the accounts of the establishment, receives his master's pay, disburses it, and will endeavour to prevent any one from cheating you but himself.

To these domestics are added, *dooreahs*, or dog boys, where people keep dogs; *chowkeydars*, or private constables, who patrol the grounds during the night; *manjies* and *dandies*, where a boat is kept; *coolies*, to carry burdens; and *hookah burdars*, or preparers of the hookah—an office which is gradually becoming extinct under the modern passion for cigars.

We here give the titles which the domestics bear at Calcutta. At Madras and Bombay there are the same classes, but under different denominations. Thus the *khansumah* is at Bombay a "*butler*," and at Madras a *dobash.* The *khetmutghar* is elsewhere called a "boy," corruption of *bhaiee*—brother. The *bheestie* at the other Presidencies is denominated a *puckauly.* The *syce* becomes a *gora-wallah* (horse-fellow) at Bombay, and a *ghirra-wallah* at Madras. The *sircar* is designated a *purvoe* at Bombay, and the *bearers* are there called *hammals*, an old Moorish word for "porters."

As none of these servants eat of the food cooked for Europeans, they are upon a uniform system of wages, which, though small as regards each individual, make up a tremendous aggregate. Not less than 200 rupees per mensem will pay the establishment of a man of large income, blessed with a family; for several ayahs, several peons, several syces and bearers, &c., have to be retained.

The lowest establishment with which a person can rub on consists of one khetmutghar or boy, one cook, and one musalchee; whose united wages, at either Presidency, will amount to between 16 and 20 rupees per month, or 25*l.* per annum. The lowest rate at which a very small house (unfurnished) may be obtained is 360 rupees, or 30*l.* per annum; and that not always in a very desirable situation. Cotton clothes, the general wear, are cheap in India, because the supply from England of piece goods is generally much in excess of the demand. Woollen clothes, on the other hand, are dear, for the tailors demand high prices for the manufacture of coats, waistcoats, and trowsers. Hats are dear; and boots of English and French manufacture are likewise costly. Excellent boots are, however, made of country leather by bootmakers on the spot, and they cost about half the price of European boots.

The style of life in India corresponds, as regards the table, with that in vogue at home. The breakfast hour is generally from 8 to 9 A.M. Tea or coffee, bread, butter, rice, fish, eggs or curries, cold meats, jams, honey or marmalade, grace the breakfast table. Soups, fish, roast, boiled, stewed, broiled, and curried meats, pastry, game, jellies, blancmange, &c., constitute the dinners. The only distinctive feature of the Indian table is the superiority and variety of the curries and the pilaus. A dish called *kitchri*—a compound of rice, split peas, fried onions, chillies, small raisins, and curried fowl or mutton—is a favourite breakfast dish. Instead of lamb, kid, the flesh of the young goat, is much esteemed. It is small, tender, and nutritious, and admits of being roasted or cut up into cutlets.

Meat bears a very low price in India compared with what is paid in England, although the markets or bazaars (especially of Calcutta) are supplied with beef, mutton, and veal, scarcely inferior to the produce of our native country. From twopence to threepence per pound is usually paid for the best kind of meat. Poultry abounds in India. Turkeys are expensive, ranging from 7 to 10 rupees each. Geese, ducks, fowls, and pigeons, are always obtainable, and at very moderate prices. The game obtainable at the Presidencies amounts to partridge, teal, snipe, wild duck, and occasionally venison; but it is never good for much. If eaten soon after it is killed, it is tough and tasteless; if kept till it becomes tender, it is often uneatable.

The vegetable and fruit market is sufficiently stocked to merit a separate chapter. Bread, composed of good wheat flour, is very cheap; rice, ditto. Milk of a thin quality abounds; but everybody desirous of being well supplied in this respect will keep his own cow. Home-made butter is preferable to that which is purchased.

For all the extras and luxuries of the table, the Indian resident is, in a great measure, indebted to England, France, and America. York and Westphalia hams, rein-deer tongues, cheeses of all kinds, hermetically sealed vegetables and fish, anchovies and sardines, potted meats, German sausages, pickles, preserved fruits—all the stock to be found at Fortnum and Mason's—may be purchased at the "Europe shops" in India. Still, a good supply of delicacies is of indigenous manufacture. The mango and lime pickles, guava and other jellies, dried fish, buffalo humps, chetney sauce, and similar condiments, are always obtainable; and from China are received large stores of ginger and other preserves, teas, sugar-candy, &c.

To Europe also the Anglo-Indian owes all his beer, wines, and spirits, paying for them less, perhaps, than he would pay in the aggregate in England, because they do not bear the same heavy duty. The beers and pale ales of Hodgson, Bass, and Allsop, and the stout of the famous Guinness, are in great request in India. The quantity of these grateful beverages which some men will drink in a single day is almost fabulous. The price of a bottle of beer, if bought in bottles by the dozen, is on an average 1*s.* 3*d.*; less, if you buy a cask and bottle it yourself. Wines lose nothing by their trip to India. Madeira gains. Even champagne and claret are to be had in considerable perfection; and the best Cognac is procurable at half the price it costs in Great Britain. Hollands, rum, whiskey, and liqueurs, are carried to India in great quantities; and even Constantia, Marsala, Tinto, and all the Rhenish wines, find a large market at the Presidencies. Soda-water is made by the chemists and provisioners of India; but nothing else in the shape of a beverage suited to Europeans is manufactured in the East.

No one who is fond of fish will find himself subject to very severe privations in India. The harbour of Bombay abounds with *pomfret*—a species of flat fish of so exquisite a flavour, that it has been reported of a celebrated *gourmand* that he thought it well worth a voyage to India—soles, seer (a large fish of the turbot flavour), bummelows (a glutinous fish of the substance of white bait, preferable when dried), prawns, hilsa (the salmon of India), and the rock fish. The Ganges, the Indus, and Irrawaddee, yield bekhtee, mullet, whiting, the *tupsee*—a delicious little fish resembling the smelt, and called the mangoe-fish, because it makes its appearance at the same time with the fruit so termed—oysters, lobsters, crawfish, and an infinite number of diminutive members of the finny tribe.

So much for the solids and fluids which go to the sustenance of civilized man in the far East.

The order—the routine, so to speak, of European life in India is unavoidably uniform and monotonous. People rise very early—before the dawn of day—for dawn and twilight are of brief duration in India; and when the sun is once "up," we begin to experience his influence. An hour's exercise, either on horseback or afoot, is supposed to be necessary to ensure the healthy action of the liver. Returning home, a bath, which literally consists in having jars of water poured over the body, is taken, the newspaper is read, and everybody proceeds to business of some kind or other; while ladies, defying the sun, sally forth in their carriages to pay visits and make purchases.

The coachmakers in Calcutta turn out vehicles scarcely inferior in appearance to some of the best productions of Long Acre. They consist chiefly of britzkas, landaulettes, buggies, chariots, and broughams, and a nondescript class of oblong and square carriages of all sizes, which rejoice in the appellations of brownberries and palkee-gharrees—from their resemblance to a palankeen on wheels; and which latter at Madras are called shigrams, and at Bombay shigrampoes.

From ten in the morning until five in the evening, everybody is at work. In the major part of the places of business at the Presidencies, the heads, foremen, and principal clerks are either Europeans or East Indians; the name given to the class who have descended from English fathers, and Mussulman or Hindoo mothers, or from the early Portuguese conquerors who formed honourable (or other) connections with native females. In the middle of the day some persons take *tiffin*, as luncheon is called; and this, in too many instances, is a sort of miniature dinner, when stews and curries are devoured, washed down by copious draughts of pale ale.

A bath and a change of dress precede the evening ride or drive. Everywhere there are strands, courses, beaches, where the denizens congregate to gossip or listen to the music of military bands. Night closes in, and the gay groups separate to return home and dine.

This is a sketch of every day *English* life, but of course it is varied by the seasons and the ordinary usages of society. There is much interchange of dinner-giving, balls are frequent at private houses, and military messes. Billiards and cards furnish excitement to great numbers; a few persons cultivate music, and now and then an amateur play, a discharge of fireworks, at the expense of some rich native, a regatta, or a *nautch* (native dance), enliven society. The races are also a great source of amusement, for most people having access to the race-course during the "trials" and training of the horses, become cognizant of their powers, and interested in their success. There is little or no trickery on the Indian turf, and the actual races, which last for a fortnight, the running taking place on alternate days, bring together all classes of society bent upon amusement. The horses which come to the post, are Arabs, country-breds, and the produce of the Cape of Good Hope. The Arab, from his small and delicate structure, and the shortness of his stride, carries the lowest weight; the country-bred carries a stone more; and the Cape horse, two stone more. English horses are seldom allowed to run, for it has been found, that, even with three or four stone greater weight upon their back than any other class of horse can bear, they win the race in a canter, owing chiefly to their length of stride. As elsewhere stated, there is some jackall hunting carried on in Calcutta, and a little shooting in the immediate neighbourhood of Bombay. Jaunts to places of interest—old temples, manufactories, curious ruins, picturesque localities, where the scramble and make-shift of a pic-nic impart excitement to the scene—are by no means unusual, and those who are fond of yachting find ample entertainment when the weather is fine and settled.

Yet, after all, the principal amusement of the English exile—his solace when all other things fail—is to be found in literature, of which, happily, there is never an insufficient supply. The local press teems with publications. There are four daily, and three or four weekly papers published in Calcutta, which, besides containing all the local intelligence, and the news from every part of the country, abound in interesting extracts from the English papers and magazines, which reach India by every mail. At Madras there are several papers published three times a week and weekly. At Bombay they have a daily and a few weekly papers. At every station throughout India are book clubs and libraries. Calcutta boasts an immense public library, to which access is easy, and at each Presidency are learned societies, whose shelves groan under the weight of ponderous volumes of Asiatic and European lore. Then there are booksellers without number, and so vast a quantity of the cheaper literature finds its way to India, that it is by no means uncommon to be assailed in your palankeen (at Calcutta at least), with offers of albums and scrapbooks, Railway Libraries, Shilling Series, Travellers' Companions, Household Words, &c., &c., which fellows nearly nude will sell you for half the London prime cost. All these resources combine to cheat the exile of much of the wearisomeness of existence; and if they be not enough, abundance of opportunities of employing time usefully are offered in the numerous associations for charitable and other purposes, which have been formed by the enterprise, philanthropy, and public spirit of Europeans. Of these, some account will be found in a subsequent chapter.

Life in the Mofussil, or interior of India, is not, perhaps, so much variegated as life at the Presidencies. Still, at the larger military stations there is no lack of such gaiety as the presence of two or three regiments invariably affords to persons fond of field sports; there are *agrémens* which are vainly sought by the denizens of the large towns. Even at the purely civil stations, where there is no regiment, the days pass in useful occupation, for the collector, the magistrate, the judge, and their assistants, have a world of work to get through, leaving them very little time for indulgence in the chase. The post is carried all over India, to the most remote stations, and to places most difficult of access. All the enjoyments, therefore, derivable from correspondence, the "news," and new books, are patent to the resident up the country. Even the indigo planter, isolated as he seems, is not without his share of joys. His business is not irksome, although it has its anxieties. When the plant has been sown, Nature does the rest, and the only grounds of solicitude on the part of the planter, are the possibility of an inundation, a heavy fall of rain, which may wash the dye entirely out of the plant, or intelligence of a glutted indigo market in England. These subjects of anxiety set aside, the indigo planter leads an easy life. He is generally something of a farmer, and not a little of a sportsman. He is the owner of horses, dogs, cows, goats, sheep, and an elephant or two. His horses are useful in enabling him to ride over his estate and watch the progress of the shrubs; his elephants are also useful for this purpose, and will carry him when out on a tiger hunt. Possibly his nearest European neighbour may reside twenty or forty miles distant. What cares the planter? He has a strong buggy, perhaps of his own building, and in three or four hours he is at a friend's door. The local papers reach him daily, and between them and the society of his little family (if he has one), or his chums and assistants, the payment of his people, the superintendence of his vats (tanks for the extraction of the dye), and the settlement of some suits at law into which he has been driven by the obstinacy or hostility of some neighbouring zemindar, or farmer, he contrives to kill time. He could scarcely be more fully employed in the busiest town.

The following very rough sketch was handed to the writer of these pages some few years ago. It is a hasty and somewhat coarse picture of the life of a prosperous planter, but its general truth is undeniable. It came from the hand of one, a genuine Irishman, all heart and animation, who sketched his own career. The "town" of which he speaks, is Calcutta, which in the cold season (November to March), is the rendezvous of all who have indigo to sell for shipment to England and elsewhere.

"The indigo planter is a hale, hearty, rollicking, kind-hearted, jovial soul, hospitable to a degree, always ready to serve a friend, and never happy but when he has his house full of them, or his friends' friends, to partake of his good fare. What a happy fellow the planter is when he comes to town with his bumper crop of *fine blue,* the favourite mark of the brokers! How happy every one is to see him, and how happy is he to see every one! Let us follow the planter to Tulloh and Co.'s Horse Bazaar. Do you see that ruddy-faced, broad-shouldered, good-humoured looking fellow, with a broad-brimmed hat, shawl-pattern waistcoat, and green shooting-coat, into the ample pocket of which he has just thrust his brawny left-hand, whilst with the right he grasps the delicate hand of a pale-faced merchant's clerk, who seems to quake under the vice-like squeeze of his hardy friend? That's Morgan Rattler, Esq., of Luckygunge concern; he is one of the fortunate planters; he only arrived in town yesterday, has just had an interview with his agents, who all rose to receive him and give him a hearty shake of the hand to congratulate him on his splendid turn out; they informed him that the brokers had been looking on his muster cakes, and Messrs. Fidong and Snaley were mad after the batch for the French market. Tiffin was at this time most opportunely announced, and for the first time in his life he was invited to step up-stairs and take a bit of beef-steak and a glass of beer, which, by the way, he consumed at such a rate as made his bilious hosts to stare again. See with what a good-natured entreating countenance he continues to grasp the trembling hand of his sallow companion! What can he be saying to him so very earnestly? Let us approach, and for once play the eaves-dropper.

"'Hut-tut, man, don't be after making a fool of yourself! Here it's as plain as a pike-staff, you can stand it no longer; you're dying by inches, man, at that horrid desk of yours; ask for leave of absence, man, and come along up with me; and if I don't put some flesh on those *aguish* bones of yours, and some colour into your faded cheeks, why, my name is not Rattler There is plenty of room in my boat, an' you need take nothing in life with you, but yourself; sure it's at Luckygunge, you'll find the best of everything. And hark ye! you must make up your mind to stay for the *chevo* I'm going to give on Saint Patrick's day in the mornin'; and won't I invite some pretty boys to meet you!'

"The planter, after eight or ten months of mixed toil and pleasure, comes to town at the close of a prosperous season with a joyous heart, professedly to eat beef and get rid of some superfluous cash; he takes up his quarters at Spence's, or Wilson's (the principal hotels), where he has a good opportunity of doing both; but the month which he allows himself for the above purpose, he perceives with regret is, like Bob Acre's courage, fast oozing out, so he orders his general storekeeper to send off his stores, and recommends him to be particularly careful about the quality of the champagne, 'for sure, didn't the fate of the next season depend entirely on the pop of the first bottle opened on the first day of manufacturing?' He despatches a few fresh Arabs, and some additions to his kennel; and now, having feasted, and been fêted, having made a speech at the planters' annual dinner, at the town hall, and sung a song at the horticultural dinner; having disbursed a few gold mohurs to some of the knowing ones at the races; having visited Wilson's saloon on Christmas morning, and purchased a slice of the mother of cakes; having given a champagne tiffin to his friends; in fact, having seen all that was possible to be seen, and done all that it was possible to do in so short a space of time, the planter proceeds to take leave of his agents, preparatory to his leaving town. As he is quitting the office, a bundle of papers carefully folded and tied with red tape, is put into his hands by one of the clerks; it is his account current, exhibiting a net profit on last year's turn-out of Co.'s rupees 80,536-8-9. And now he is

The Government Buildings, Madras.

off to his own element, the Mofussil. Let us go along with him and see him in his glory.

"We'll suppose Morgan Rattler, Esq., arrived at Luckygunge, where, as he approaches his handsome and elegantly furnished mansion, he is met by his gomasta-jee and a whole host of sircars, all bowing and salaaming, and each anxious to catch a glance from their master's eye; he makes some inquiries about the factory, the state of the October crop, and the fate of such or such a civil suit that has been going on for the last six years. He then turns to his jemadar syce (or head groom), and makes most affectionate inquiries after the health and well-being of his horses and dogs. Having said a kind word to each, he gives them all their *rooksut*. And now approaches his favourite, the garrulous English writer, Rajnarain, with his 'good moren, sare; hope master is well in health; many letters for master.' 'Hah! are there?—from whom?' 'Oh, from different, indifferent gentlemens, master's friends, who all will be much glad to hear master come back.' 'Ay, ay, here they are, sure enough: what a precious set of correspondents I have, to be sure! Here's from Snooks, and Shanks, and Brown, and Snaggs, and Sniggers, and—oh! here's a chit from young Never-do-good; let's see what he has to say for himself:—

"'My Dear Rattler,—Glad you're back again; we had capital sport yesterday; such a run, and my eye, such spilling! oh, you ought to've been with us; there never was such fun; made seven grunters bite the dust; I had a most awful purl myself; went slap-bang into a khate; snapped off my mare's leg—obliged to shoot her on the spot, poor thing! Oh, hang it, never mind, I'll replace her with half a dozen Arabs, if I make a good season, and old Blowhard, my gomasta, assures me that we're sure to do so. Come over, man, or by Jove we 'll storm you, to give you a benefit. We 're to have a grand rifle match in a day or two. Old Snarleyyow is floored at last. Just heard of a grunter being in the neighbourhood, so I 'm off.—Yours to the last grunt,

'NEWMAN NOGGS.'

"The life of an indigo planter is decidedly the most delightful one in India; much, however, depends on the first set off. The getting connected with a good concern at the first start, is the tide in the affairs of the planter, which taken at the flood, leads on to fortune, &c. How perfectly independent he feels, and really is, in the Mofussil! with what awe and respect he is looked upon by the ryots around him! To whom does the miserable, hard-worked, ill-fed ryot, in his hour of trouble, flee for protection, aye, even for protection against the unfair and oppressive acts of his own countryman, the native talookdar? To whom but to the kind-hearted and generous planter, the *ma bap,* as they style him, of the locality? And seldom does he apply in vain, for the planter has a heart that can feel for another, and thus, in endeavouring to do good to all around him, his days run peacefully on, unless he has the misfortune to have a *budzat* of a neighbour to steal his coolies, and offer higher rents for his lands as their *pottahs* (leases) expire.

"The planter rises in the morning with the lark; he passes through a lane of obsequious, well-dressed servants, and receives a salaam down to the ground from each as he makes his way to the veranda where the khansamah awaits him, chowrie in hand, to keep off the flies from his master's coffee. On a tea-tray beside him rests the last newspaper which came in during the night; there are also letters, some from his *real,* and some from his 'faithful' friends; he runs his eye over them, and then turns to a fresh chapter of the last new novel; meantime his beautiful Arab is ready saddled, being led up and down the avenue before his admiring eyes, and his dogs caper about and make the welkin ring with their loud baying. The gomasta approaches with a handful of native letters from the out-factories; some announcing rain and the completion of the sowings, some asking for cash, &c. Answers are directed to be prepared for each, and then the light-hearted planter jumps into the saddle, and his noble steed springs forward with its curved neck and flowing tail; he passes over fields of indigo, and his eyes are gladdened at the sight of such flourishing plants. And now he ventures to make a mental calculation of the probable profit that—barring all accidents—may accrue therefrom. As he continues his ride, turning duty into pleasure, he sees his people at work around him, and receives a '*salaam kodawund*' from each as he passes; he has no fault to find with anybody; everything *chulls* (goes on) like clockwork, and so, after one or two smart runs after a jackall or fox, with a contented heart he turns his horse's head homewards. Arrived, he throws himself upon a damask couch, or easy chair, and takes up his favourite paper, to finish some pleasant editorial contained therein. And now approaches his faithful sirdar-bearer to inform his lord that the *hazree ka woquet* (breakfast time) has arrived; and as the planter is about to retire to dress, rat-a-plat, rat-a-plat, come galloping up the avenue half a dozen flannel-jacketed and *solah**-hatted planters, and their assistants. Rattler runs into the veranda to give his friends a hearty welcome, and in an instant has his right arm nearly dislocated by the force with which his visitors try at it in their *empressement* to welcome him back with a hearty, true old English shake of the hand.

* The *solah* is a white pulp of a tree, of a light texture, admirably adapted to keep off the sun's rays.

"'Well, Rattler, my boy, I'm as glad as twopence to see you back again.'

"'Ha! Snooks, how goes it? eh? *Comment vous*—how do you do, Monsieur Sangfroid? Delighted to see you.'

"'Ha! Mister Rattailer—my goodness it is very estrange—*je ne peut jamais achever un compliment en Anglais; merci*, Monsieur Rattleir, I am moosh glad to see you back; PAR *bleu*, dat will do I tink!'

"'Oh, Rattler! we had such a flare up at Noggs's the other day, but we wanted you, man—we wanted you; have you heard of old Snarley's misfortune?'

"'But I say, Sniggers, don't you feel rather comflushed after last night's booz? Hi, Kudda Bux, *bellattee pawny lao.*' *

"'*Acha kodahwund*," † and in a brace of minutes a dozen of Bathgate's double-aërated are made marines of.

"Breakfast is now over, the lamb chops and sauterne have been tried and pronounced excellent, and now for the order of the day.

"'Well, my boys, what shall we be after? Snooks, I know, will be for the billiards; let Shanks go along with him, and you, Mr. Cunningfellow, you had better follow and look on and learn, and let those who choose, take a stroll with me into the stables. I want to look after my purchases, after which we'll have a set-to with the rifles or quoits, or whatever you like best.'

"Thus passes the day, during which *bellattee pawny* is in constant requisition. Allsopp's pale ale has been opened by dozens at a time, and hundreds, nay thousands of Manillas have been puffed into the air.

"The sun is now declining in the western hemisphere, and the jolly host reminds his guests that the horses

* "Bring soda-water!"

† "Yes, sir;" or—"Good, your slave will do it."

and elephant are ready at the door; a hasty wash and change of clothes now takes place, and behold our friends mounted and dashing on to the highlands in search of a jackall, or whatever fortune may throw in their way. * * * *

"It is night, and a hundred lights illume the mansion; the bearded khansumah, with folded hands, informs his *munnib* that *kannah* (dinner) is on the table. We will not say one hackneyed word about the choicest viands of the season, sparkling wines, groans of the table, and all that kind of thing; suffice it to say, Morgan Rattler was never known to give a bad dinner, and so now that we have got his guests' legs under his mahogany, let us leave them to get from under it when, and how, they can.

"It must not be supposed that the life of a planter is always *couleur de rose*. Oh, no! the dark clouds of adversity and disappointment obscure the horizon of the planter as they do that of all other walks in life; the season may be unfavourable, perhaps downright bad, much money has been sunk, lost, because of a few showers of rain more or less; and then the agents hum and haw, and look stiff, and talk about low prices, scarcity of money in the market, panic at home, crisis in America, hostilities with France, necessity of curtailment, &c. &c. But all this kind of thing does not make the planter despair: he exclaims with Jacob Faithful, 'Better luck next time,' believes in the hope of doing better next year, and when the next season is closed, and his hopes have been realized beyond all computation, who would, or could, grudge him his good luck? Let us rather close this long yarn by wishing each good fellow among the fraternity a bumper season this year, and many duplicates of it for the future."

The life of an English lady in India is one of perfect leisure. No household cares occupy her thoughts or kill her time. The *khansumah* and the *ayah* between them assume all the duties which in England pertain to the mistress of a household, and she has little left her to do beyond reading the stock of a circulating library, and doing a little knitting and crochet work. If she be an equestrian, and is so circumstanced as to have horses kept for her, the early mornings and late evenings may be consumed in out-of-door exercise—if she is musical, or cultivates the fine arts, a part of the day may be pleasantly employed in illustrating the scenery of the country, and the costumes and habits of the people. If piously or charitably inclined, or disposed to activity in the absence of ennobling motives, the numerous ladies' committees of the branches of the Bible societies, or associations for the promotion of education among the Christian poor or native females, open a scope to her philanthropy. Should she happily be a mother of children, the *baba logue*, or little people, as the olive-branches are called in India, engage much of her care, and mitigate the solitude of her position, while her husband is engaged in his official duties.

Children, though a source of much delight in India, are, at the same time, objects of great solicitude. Prematurely enfeebled by the intense heat of the climate, and exposed to all the diseases incidental to infancy in other countries, they either grow up poor attenuated creatures, or are sent to England, ere they attain their sixth year, that their constitutions may not be shaken irrevocably. In either case the parents endure much agony. They must either see their offspring waste away and fall victims to disease, or consent to be separated from them for many years, to the utter destruction of all those sentiments which hallow the relations of parent to child, and constitute the chief charm of existence. It is rare indeed that, after a separation of five or six years, a son or daughter sufficiently remember their parents to feel towards them the affection which is the result of perpetual intercourse. A sad drawback is all this to the pleasure of matrimony in India, but it is an evil without remedy. There are certainly schools and sanataria in the mountains of India, access to which is comparatively easy, and where the fierceness of the sun is mitigated and subdued by the fine breezes from the north; but the quality of education at the academies, and the continual companionship of native servants, are unfavourable to the formation of that peculiarly "British" character which every Englishman holds to be desirable in his child. Separation therefore becomes unavoidable. The addition of a child or two makes an enormous difference in the expenditure of a family, for there must be special servants to attend upon them. There must be a nurse, and often a little boy, and when the hope of the family is two or three years old, he must have a pony wherewith to take the air, and the pony must have a syce. Then the doctor of the establishment is more frequently called in to assuage a mother's alarm, and bills increase in length. It is only in the article of dress that children are inexpensive. For the greater part of the day their clothing consists of one small chemise, and they are neither encumbered with stockings nor shoes. Their toys are not costly, for the India manufacturers compose them either of wood or *sola*—the light pulp of a tree;—the former cannot be broken, and the latter are so cheap, that if one hundred per week were immolated, a father could hardly feel the loss.

# CHAPTER VI.

## TRAVELLING IN INDIA.

*The first railway—Boat travelling on the Ganges—The banks of the Hooghly—Dawk—Marching—The necessary preparations and equipment.*

It will scarcely be credited by those who know the English propensity to improve every possession, reclaim every inch of savage ground, and augment the comforts of the inhabitants of any country under their rule, how little has been done to promote intercourse with the interior by the construction of carriage roads. There are but one or two good long roads, extending across the continent, over which a buggy may be safely driven—the rest are paths cut by the continual traffic of native carts, pedestrians, camel *cafilas*, or caravans, and the dawk. Had it not been that a railway has just been opened in a corner of India, between Bombay and Tannah, this little volume would have gone forth, with the announcement, so discreditable to the rulers of the country, that although we have had railways in England since 1827, and have constructed them in the West Indies and other colonies, such a means of locomotion was still wanting in the East Indies. The event—the opening of the Bombay and Tannah railway—is one of such deep interest and importance, heralding, as we may hope it does, a still greater advance in that direction, that we shall make no apology for transferring the description of the ceremony from the fugitive pages of the *Illustrated News*.

The time-honoured maxim, that peace has its triumphs as well as war, has just been exemplified in Western India by the opening of the Great Indian Peninsula railway, on the 16th of April, 1853, which must be a memorable day henceforth in the annals of the country—memorable as the greatest of battles, and surely more glorious. The interesting intelligence is recorded with glowing enthusiasm by the Bombay journals. The *Overland Telegraph* and *Courier* describes the above event as "a triumph, to which, in comparison, all our victories in the East seem tame and commonplace. The opening of the Great Indian Peninsula railway will be remembered by the natives of India when the battle fields of Plassey, Assaye, Meanee, and Goojerat, have become the mere landmarks of history. The proud arrays of England have conquered, and kept in subjection, hundreds of millions of people, but her power was never so nobly exemplified as when, upon the above date, the long line of carriages, conveying nearly 500 persons, glided smoothly and easily away amidst the shouts of assembled thousands. It was then that the immense masses of the native population paid true and heartfelt homage to the power and greatness of their European conquerors. The superstition of ages seemed to melt away as the gigantic reality of steam and mechanism passed before their wondering eyes. A locomotive engine conveys an idea of calm concentrated power. There is no straining at starting: a touch is given, the wheels revolve, and the immense mass rolls on without trembling or undulation. The natives saw this, and they salaamed the omnipotence of steam as it passed.

Before we describe the ceremony of the day, we shall sketch the railway itself. The first turf was turned at Bombay, on the 31st of October, 1850. Very little was done for the first eight months, till Messrs. Faviell and Fowler, the contractors, at one end, and Mr. Jackson at the other, took matters in hand. The work appears to have been one of great labour and difficulty. In addition to a most trying climate (in which the constitution of Mr. Fowler, the partner of Mr. Faviell, as well as that of many of the English labourers they took out with them, failed), Mr. Faviell found himself, in March, 1852, working single-handed, his partner having gone to England for the benefit of his health. Mr. Faviell was then dependent principally on native labour: the men are scarce, and in the rice-harvest time always difficult to manage: alteration in the arrangement of the work, or strict orders given by the contractor, often gave offence, when men went away in a body of fifty or a hundred at a time. It was also difficult to get them to earn their small rate of wages.

Snakes abounded on the line: the cobra di capello, and a small dark snake, were very common among the stones; the former is an object of worship, and both have a deadly bite. Under these and many other difficulties, however, the double line of railway has been completed from Bombay to Tannah.

From the Boree Bunder the railway proceeds by a very densely-peopled district, till, skirting along the shore, it passes the lofty precipice of Nowrojee Hill. Here the public road twice crosses it at nearly right angles, where huge gates shut up the railway, or cut off the public road, according as they are in one position or another. After passing under the Mazagon viaduct, opposite the Suddur Awlut, the railway describes a graceful double curve of large radius, and then crosses the Byculla road, near the Bishop's house, and, passing under a viaduct, it reaches the flats near the race-course. From the curious gravel-bank called Phipps's Cart, it stretches along the flats to Sion for six miles, in almost a straight line. At Sion it passes under the public road and along the base of the hill, on the summit of which is an old Marathi fort, and a Portuguese church contiguous. Here it is joined by the branch at Mahim, an unimportant fishing village, but likely to be transformed by the railway into a busy port. Next, the line sweeps across the Sion Marsh, the embanking of which threatened to be very troublesome—the material thrown in sinking amongst the mud, which afterwards rose up, forming a little island on each side along the line. Here, immediately adjoining, and nearly parallel to the railway, we have the Sion causeway on one side; and full in view, two miles distant, the magnificent work of the like kind, constructed by Sir Jamsetjee Jejeebhoy, and first opened in 1844. The railway now bends considerably to the right, and, passing through a long line of salt-pans, it enters Salsette, and encounters the only formidable obstruction on the line—a beautifully wooded ridge, traversed by an open cutting, about a mile and a half in length, about one hundred and twenty feet across at the widest part, and fifty feet in depth. For the next fourteen miles the line is perfectly level, the rails being laid along the surface of the ground with merely sufficient embanking to save them from the risk of flooding during the rains. The country, for a considerable distance, is open on both sides, and the view is extremely beautiful. To the left are the low, rocky, wooded ridges of Salsette; woodlands and richly-cultivated fields, hamlets and cottages, filling up the intervening space. On the right, parallel to and close beside the railway for about eight miles, is the salt-water creek called the Tannah River, and just beyond are the magnificent ghauts. The line, on approaching Tannah, becomes embowered under magnificent trees. On entering the village, it turns rather quickly round towards the viaduct, by which it crosses the river, here divided by a long and rocky island. The channel on the Tannah side is narrow, and the arches here are of moderate span. On the mainland side the channel is deep and narrow; and an iron bridge, somewhat on the tubular plan, 86 feet span, permits the shipping to pass under it. The whole viaduct, from shore to shore, including the part over the river, is about 1,000 feet in length, and the ferry way about 40 feet above the high-water mark. Thence the line runs along the base of the hill, at a distance of about three miles, right on to the projecting spur of Parsick Point, which it penetrates by a tunnel of 100 yards in length. On the other side the traveller passes for about a mile along the margin of the Callian River, surrounded by some of the most magnificent scenery in the world, when a second tunnel is passed, and the village of Callian is soon reached.

The inauguration, on the 16th of April, was altogether a most interesting scene. By half-past three o'clock the majority of the company had taken their seats in the train.

The state carriage was occupied by Sir William and Lady Yardley, Sir Charles and Lady Jackson, the Hon. A. Bell and Lady, the Hon. D. A. Blane, Sir Henry and Lady Leeke, &c.

At half-past three o'clock, a royal salute was fired from the ramparts of Fort George, immediately after which the well-filled train, consisting of fourteen first, second, and third-class carriages, drawn by three locomotive engines, and containing in all, it was said, above five hundred persons, started for the terminus at Boree Bunder.

Tens of thousands of persons surrounded the spot;

and, as the moving mass swept along the way, still there were tens of thousands looking on—men, women, and children—perched on wall tops, on the branches of trees, even on the masts of Arab buglas along the harbour; from windows and from the tops of temples and of houses; from every eminence around the town: finally, when the train had passed the more densely-populated parts, still the surrounding fields were studded with spectators.

Besides the inhabitants of Bombay proper, and the neighbouring country, there were in those crowds people from Scinde, from Cabul, from Affghanistan, from Central Asia, from the Persian Gulf, from Arabia, and from the East Coast of Africa.

There is little to describe, particularly to the great majority of our readers, in an ordinary railway trip. It is due, however, to those who had the task of maturing all the arrangements for the occasion, to say that everything went on smoothly. The train stopped at Sion, going out, to allow of the engines being watered. At no time was the speed above thirty-five miles an hour, and generally it was much under that. On the train approaching Tannah, the crowds lined the sides thickly for more than a mile, and were kept in order by the Ghat police. The time taken to reach Tannah (twenty-four miles), including the stoppage at Sion, was fifty-five minutes. The return trip occupied only forty.

Arrived at Tannah, the party found, under an immense tent, at once a cool retreat and a splendid tiffin. Major Swanson, the senior Director present, took the chair; supported by the Hon. Sir William Yardley, Chief Justice; by Sir Henry Leeke, R.N., Commander-in-Chief of the Indian Navy; also immediately surrounded by the Hon. Messrs. Bell and Blane, Members of Council; Sir Charles Jackson, Puisne Judge H. M.'s Supreme Court; Colonel F. P. Lester,

Surgeon - General Taylor, Superintending - Surgeon Boyd, Colonel Woodburn, C.B., Commandant of the Garrison; Mr. Le Messurier, Advocate - General; Colonel Hale, Adjutant-General; and a distinguished company, comprising the *élite* of Bombay.

At a separate table laid out for the Parsee passengers were Messrs. Cursetjee Jamsetjee, Bomanjee Hormusjee, Manockjee Nusserwanjee, Merwanjee Jeejeebhoy, Sorabjee Jamsatjee, Limjee Manockjee, Furdoonjee Hormasjee, Nowrojee Furdoonjee, Nowrojee Dorabjee Chabookwalla. Sitting quietly looking on were Meer Ali Jan and a few Marwarrie gentlemen.

Several appropriate speeches were made, and toasts drunk, which we have not space to report.

Shortly after, the party broke up, and returned to the Boree Bunder terminus.

As it must necessarily be some years before railways can become general in India, we must altogether put them out of consideration for the present in treating of the mode of travelling open to the Europeans and respectable natives in that country.

The only methods, then, by which remote distances can be reached are the boat, the dawk, and the horse.

Boat travelling is common on the Ganges, the Indus, the Brahmapootra, and the Irrawaddy. The other rivers, such as the Nerbudda, the Godavery, Kistna, &c., admit of traffic by small boats, but are rarely traversed by Europeans.

The boat travelling is of two kinds. There is the accommodation flat, tugged by iron steamers on the Ganges, and proceeding as far as the Jumna, and there is the barge, or schooner, under the various denominations of budgerow, pinnace, and bholio. The budgerow is the largest, and for a person who is not in a hurry, it forms a very agreeable mode of transit. The larger budgerows are of from fifty to eighty tons burthen. One-half of the vessel consists of a decked cabin having two or three spacious rooms, a poop, and an awning. The fore part of the vessel is occupied by the crew, who consist of a manjee, or steersman, and from six to ten dandies, or boatmen, who either work the sails, or row or tug the vessel when the wind and tide are adverse. The budgerow is often accompanied by a *panshway*, a small boat in which the cooking is carried on, for it is impossible to exist in the bungalow cabin if cooking is conducted on board with the wind ahead. In these budgerows voyages are made into the interior to a distance of 1,000 miles, occupying two, three, and even four months. A gentleman, therefore, must take with him his establishment of servants—at any rate, his cook and his personal servant. Fowls, milk, and butter, can be obtained at the villages on the banks of the river, and rice and fire-wood are also to be had; but anything else must be carried from Calcutta. Thus a store of hams, tongues, humps, preserved meats, anchovies, sardines, pickles, preserves, &c., will be found necessary, and a complete camp equipage is indispensable. With a few books and an intelligent companion a river voyage is by no means so disagreeable a thing. The banks of the river present a variety of scenery, and when the wind is foul, or the budgerow gets upon a sand-bank, the passenger can go on shore and amuse himself with his fowling-piece.

To one who has never seen any larger river than the Thames or Severn, the Ganges presents a noble appearance. Its immense expanse raises the idea of an ocean; the distant trees look more as if they grew on detached islands than on the opposite bank of the river. The stillness of the scene adds to the illusion; for notwithstanding the rapid current and muddy tinge of the water, the Ganges flows on so soft and yielding a soil that it is accompanied by none of that loud hoarse murmuring which characterizes a body of water running over a rocky bed or gravelly bottom.

The Ganges, however, is very different to the Hooghly, the river which is continued from it to the ocean. The former realizes the sublime, the latter is simply pretty.

It is astonishing that so little has ever been said and written about the extraordinary beauty of the banks of the Hooghly, in the environs of Calcutta. The scenery on either side of the river is charming. The mariner who has, during a long period, gazed upon nothing excepting sky and water, must fancy that Paradise has opened upon his wondering eyes. While the upper provinces of India, though boasting grander features (the Hooghly being the most sublime object in the picture we are contemplating), present, at various seasons of the year, very different aspects, Bengal is always the same. The moisture of its climate, and the nature of the soil, concur in preserving an eternal verdure, which is only to be seen during the season of the rains in the more arid districts. Even in the hottest weather, when the thermometer is up to 130°, perhaps for weeks together, and when the sun pours down so fierce a flood of light that it would seem as if its scorching influence were sufficient to dry up every blade of grass, the whole earth is covered with a rich carpet, and the moment that the sun sets, a refreshing coolness fills the air, and the eyes revel upon scenery of the richest luxuriance. Excepting in the immediate vicinity of the river, Bengal is a dead flat; and were it not for the diversity occasioned by the quantity of its wood, sometimes spread into groves, at others thickening into forests, and in all places profusely scattered, it would be monotonous in the extreme. But the banks of the Hooghly are, in many places, so high that, especially at some sharp angle of the river, they assume the character of promontories; and these are wooded to the top. Nothing can exceed the beauty of the foliage which waves over this favoured land. The bamboo flings its long branches down with all the grace of the willow, the numerous species of palms rise in regal majesty above, and the fine feathery foliage of both are relieved by the bright masses of the neem, the peepul, and a host of others, many bearing resplendent flowers of a thousand dyes. The magnolia is common in the neighbourhood of Calcutta, and amid a vast number of the acacia tribe, there is one of peculiar beauty, called the babool. It is covered with a flower tufted like a ball, of a golden colour, which gives out so delicious a perfume to the breeze that one is sufficient to scent a whole garden.

Upon leaving Calcutta, the river, for miles, presents the most gay and beautiful scenes imaginable. At comparatively short intervals there are ghauts or landing places, built from the banks into the water, for the purpose of affording facilities for the natives to bathe and fill their water-pots; these are all constructed of brick, chunamed. The chunam is a stucco made principally of lime, which takes a fine polish, and which, being porous, always presents a dry surface. It gives all the effects of stone to the buildings which are faced with it; and when formed of the finest materials, many beautiful architectural ornaments are constructed of it. Near these ghauts, which consist of wide flights of steps finished on either side with a balustrade, there is usually a mosque, a pagoda, or a series of small Hindoo temples, entitled mhuts, which are of a bee-hive shape, and not a great deal larger, and which, when grouped together, produce a very good effect. The summits of the most striking elevations are usually crowned by a picturesque building, either a mosque or a pagoda; formerly the latter were invariably known by the mitre-like appearance of their domes, but many modern erections have the round, flattened dome of Mussulman temples. These beautiful domes, or their accompanying minarets, are sometimes only seen peeping through the branches of the trees; and if placed on high ground, they are approached by a stair, which winds down the declivity, and is partially revealed at every opening. These stairs, which are very handsome, usually end in a ghaut; and they are often, if belonging to a Hindoo temple, strewed from the top to the bottom with fresh flowers of the most beautiful description. Long garlands of the Indian jessamine, a large white double blossom, with a rich but heavy perfume—or of a large scarlet or yellow flower, hang over the rails, and are often flung into the river as propitiatory offerings; every Hindoo shrine being profusely decorated with flowers, the floors even are strewed with them. The followers of Mahomed have so far adopted the custom of their heathen neighbours, as to spread flowers upon the tombs of their departed friends; both religions light lamps in their temples at night, and the glimmering of these small beacons through the trees after sunset adds considerably to the charm of the scene. There is likewise another attraction. Many of the trees actually seem encircled by a halo, in consequence of the multitudes of fire-flies which glance in and out, emitting a greenish golden light, like that which would proceed from a lamp formed of emeralds. Though the greater number of these luminous insects disport themselves round the trees, many flash like meteors along the air, crossing the path, whether on shore or on the water, and rendering night more beautiful, even in the presence of the stars, which come out so thickly and so brightly in this glittering hemisphere, that, excepting during the cloudy season of the rains, the nights are never dark. While the sun has still left a soft stain of either saffron or crimson upon the river, how pleasant it is to glide along; at one time, a wooded promontory stretching into the water, bounding the view—at another, a wide expanse of water opening before it, studded with islands, and apparently leading to regions of still softer enchantment. All this pomp of beauty is increased as we approach Barrackpore and Serampore, places opposite to each other, on the banks of the river, sixteen miles from Calcutta.

The principal part of Barrackpore lies inland, but the ghaut, the signal-post, the viceregal palace, and various other buildings, partly embowered in trees, are visible; while on the opposite shore, Serampore presents one of the noblest esplanades that can be imagined, backed by a range of magnificent houses. Some are exceedingly lofty, and surrounded by extensive court-yards; others present rich clusters of pillars in long colonnades, supporting verandahs tier upon tier, while the number of fine trees which intervene afford a most beautiful diversity of objects. The interior of Serampore keeps the promise which a distant view has given; it is without exception the best kept town in India. The Protestant missionaries of Bengal have established their head-quarters at Serampore; there they have erected a college, one of the largest and handsomest amid the many large and handsome buildings of the place, and the Danes themselves (who formerly owned Serampore) being a highly religious and a very quiet and orderly community, there is nothing in the shape of dissipation going on in a settlement which looks as if it must belong to some splendid and brilliant court, the suburban retreat of regal magnificence. The ghauts are not crowded as in Calcutta with multitudes of merely trading vessels, but the frigate-like pinnace, the gaily-painted budgerow, and the graceful bohlio, somewhat resembling, though more brilliant in its decorations, the Venetian gondola, dance upon the glittering surface of the river, or spreading their white sails to the breeze, glide swiftly along. These gay and fairy-like vessels are contrasted by the country craft continually ascending or descending the mighty stream, boats of various dimensions, from eighty maunds burthen (a maund is about forty pounds), to the small dinghee, which looks as if the centre was formed of a hogshead, the sort of cabin or awning raised as a protection against the weather, having this appearance. The larger kinds have thatched roofs, or choppers as they are called; and they are rendered still more picturesque by a ragged sail, sometimes the colour of ochre, and by long garlands of white, yellow, and scarlet flowers, festooned from the prow.

The native groups which congregate in the streets and ghauts of Serampore are very striking. No abject poverty, and no disgusting features of any kind, are to be seen; the very convicts who work in fetters in the streets, and who are employed in removing dirt or rubbish of every sort, are cheerful and orderly. In fact, the lower orders of natives lazily reconcile themselves to their condition, and if not ill-treated will submit with patience to any change of fortune. And here it will not be out of place to introduce an anecdote relative to convicts in India that is highly characteristic of native society, and shows the extraordinary principles of honour on which even the lower classes act:—A magistrate, being anxious to cut a road through a dense forest, employed the convicts under his charge for that purpose. The labour was very great, and also exceedingly tedious, in consequence of the difficulty which the men sustained in working in their manacles. The magistrate was known to be of a benevolent disposition, and a deputation of the convicts waited on him one day, and told him that if he would permit their fetters to be removed, and trust to their pledge that they would not take advantage of the facilities it would afford them for escape, he should not lose a single man; while the work would be more speedily and efficiently performed. The magistrate, after a short deliberation, determined to hazard the chance of what might have been a very serious affair to himself, and relieved the men from their chains. Long before he could have expected its completion he had nine miles of broad road cleared; while the convicts returned voluntarily every night to their jail, and as they had promised, he did not lose one of their number.

There are a number of natives resident at Serampore. Some of their houses, having rather a castellated appearance, and being more secluded from view than those of the Europeans, may be seen half-shadowed by trees, and half abutting into the river, adding considerably to the beauty and variety of the landscape. They also assemble in huge parties in the streets and thoroughfares, all clad in the purest white muslin. The Hindoos of Bengal have not so generally adopted the Mohammedan vest and trousers as those of the upper country. They wear the dhotee, which consists of one long breadth of muslin folded round the loins, and descending in very graceful drapery to the ancles. The upper part of their bodies is only partially covered with another breadth of muslin, which is arranged in a variety of ways, the wearer often changing its mode as he walks along. Notwithstanding the fierce vertical rays of the sun, the Bengallees frequently go bareheaded, the men occasionally somewhat effeminately wearing a wreath of white flowers in their hair. The triple string, the distinguishing mark of a Brahmin, worn across the shoulder, and fastening on the opposite side at the waist, is frequently formed of threaded flowers, and has a good appearance upon the polished skins of men, who from the symmetry of their proportions may be compared to so many moving statues of bronze. Sometimes the rich people are disfigured by a superabundance of flesh, but in that case they have usually the good taste to put on additional clothing. Rich gold ornaments in the shape of bracelets, ear-rings, and talismans of various kinds suspended from the neck, complete a costume which is graceful, flowing, and picturesque. It would be difficult by mere words to convey any adequate idea of the soft enchantments of a scene in which the magnificent and the romantic are so strongly blended together.

The adoption of the budgerow in preference to the river steamer or the dawk, is generally the result of economical considerations. The fare by the river steamer is very high, and beyond the means of a young officer about to join his regiment, or an assistant planter proceeding to his factory. In the case of the officer a certain number of days are allowed him for the voyage, during which he receives a travelling gratuity in the shape of extra daily pay, and this supplies an inducement to him to take the slower course when other motives do not prevail.

Boat travelling can only be effected by those who belong to the Bengal Presidency, or who may be ordered from the mouth of the Indus to a station at the upper part of the Sutlej. In the latter case, the Bombay officer is conveyed to Kurrachee, the chief port at the mouth of the Indus, and from thence he makes his way by a river steamer or boat. The voyage up the Indus is far from pleasant. The intense heat, the sandy shores, the burning blast, carrying with it millions of particles of sand, the unfriendly character of the natives—all combine to render the voyage dreary, painful, and uninteresting.

The dawk, or palankeen conveyance, is a certain if not a rapid means of transit. Ensconced in a palankeen, borne by four natives, who are accompanied by four or eight more, to relieve them at brief intervals, you are carried up the country at the rate of something less than three miles an hour. Lying your length along upon a well-stuffed mattrass, covered with silk or morocco leather, supported by pillows, and having in front of you at the upper end of the interior of the palankeen, a shelf and drawer, and nettings containing books, a telescope, writing materials, biscuits, and a bottle of weak brandy and water, you pass over many miles delightfully enough. You stop when you please, and at intervals—arranged by yourself—you halt at a bungalow, or small building on the ground floor, which the Government has constructed for the accommodation of travellers in a country where no road-side inn offers shelter to the wayfarer. Here an active servant prepares you a breakfast, or a simple dinner of curried fowl, while a mussalchee will procure you the means of having a refreshing bath, in a room appropriated to such purposes.

You may remain, if you like, an entire day at the bungalow for the small charge of one rupee; of course, paying extra for the meals—a mere trifle. As your baggage always accompanies you, in tin boxes, covered with waterproof material, and slung across the shoulders of *bangy wallahs*, as they are called, you are enabled to procure a change of linen, to write letters of business or friendship, and to while away an hour in sketching (if you have a taste and talent for drawing) the scenery around you, which is often of a very pleasing character. To do them justice, the engineer officers, who constructed the bungalows, have selected the most interesting and elevated sites.

If a person intends to proceed into the interior by dawk, the Post-Master-General at the Presidency must receive timely intimation of his purposes, that he may give orders to the functionaries along the line of route, to order the relays of bearers to be in attendance at the time specified. At the same time the intending traveller pays to the Post-Master-General the expenses of the trip, and an additional sum, by way of deposit for demurrage—that is to say, he offers a sort of guarantee that, if he does not travel at the rate he at first intended, he will make good the sum that has been expended in retaining bearers on the line for his special use.

Dawk travelling is conducted both by night and day. At night, a mussalchee runs by the side of the palankeen with a lighted torch to guide the bearers through the jungles—which torch he continually feeds from a bottle of oil slung at his waist. To scare away wild animals and serpents, and to cheer them on their journey, the bearers often keep up a low murmuring chorus—one of them calling out a few words of a song (often *impromptu*, and not always complimentary to the traveller if he be above the average weight), and the remainder taking up the *refrain*.

A horse dawk has been established within the last few years to run between Calcutta and Delhi. It consists of a palankeen on wheels, and will perhaps become general before the railways are constructed.

A more independent, but of course a much slower mode of making one's way up the country, is to march, or rather ride on horseback, accompanied by a tent, bag, and baggage. This plan is unavoidable along the roads where a dawk has not been established, or when an officer proceeds with a detachment of troops. Rising at four or five A.M., the traveller mounts his steed and proceeds for about fifteen miles or more, while his tent either precedes or follows him. By the time the sun is high in the heavens, and his rays become intolerable, the tent has been pitched in a mango grove, breakfast prepared, the horse picketted and groomed, and the traveller refreshed with a bath. The day is then passed in shooting, reading, or perhaps in a visit to some neighbouring civilian, or planter, and bed is sought at an early hour, that the tent may be struck betimes, and conveyed to the next appointed stage.

Short distances are often accomplished by relays of horses. Men in India think nothing of riding from fifty to seventy miles without any other pause than is necessary for dismounting from one horse and mounting another. Sometimes, when the road will admit of it, a journey is made in a buggy—a sort of hooded cab. On the Bombay side of India there is a regular coach, which travels up the ghauts from Panwell, two hours' sail from Bombay, but the distance effected is very small in comparison to what ought to be accomplished in and for such a country as India.

In speaking of travelling, no reference is necessary to journeys on the summit of an elephant or a camel. No one having respect for his bones, would voluntarily adopt a species of locomotion which is invariably attended with great pain and fatigue.

# CHAPTER VII.

## THE VEGETABLE PRODUCTIONS OF INDIA.

*The Banian tree—Ganesha—The Peepul—General belief—The Sissoo—The Sygwam—The Talipot, its uses—The Cocoa-nut, invaluable to the native—Traditions of the mango grove.*

THE tropical lands are proverbially rich in vegetation. Nature has lavished upon them all her choicest gifts. The most gigantic trees, the densest forests, the broadest leaves, the largest flowers, the most luxurious creepers, luscious fruits, nutritious vegetables, herbs of overpowering fragrance, simples of inestimable efficacy—a pharmacopeia unrivalled. These are the characteristics of the spontaneous vegetation of India. Nowhere is there such abundance or such infinite variety. But man, not content with the free offerings of Nature, or anxious to recognise and expand her fertility, has employed all the resources of art to evolve the powers of the soil, and to add to the stores of the East the useful and wholesome productions of the West; while piety has laboured to increase the indigenous offspring of the land, and commerce has demanded a multiplication of those trees which enjoy favour in countries where vegetation is comparatively scant. There is nothing for which the sylvan scenery of India is more remarkable than the groves of palm and mango trees planted all over the empire—the former in the vicinity of the coasts, the latter in the north-western provinces and Behar. A strong religious feeling influences the Hindoo in these plantations. He believes that his soul in the next world is benefited by the blessings and grateful feelings of those of his fellow creatures who, unmolested, eat the fruit and enjoy the shade of the trees he has planted during his sojourn in this world. The names of the great men who built the castles, palaces, and tombs at Delhi and Agra, have been almost all forgotten, because no one enjoys any advantages from them; but the names of those who planted the mango groves are still supposed to be remembered by all who eat of their fruit, sit in their shade, and drink of their water, from whatever part of the world they come.

The most stupendous and remarkable trees in India are, the teak, the palm, the banyan, the sissoo, the saul, the peepul, the bamboo, and the talipot.

Of these, for the extent of ground which it covers, and the peculiarity of its growth, the banian, or *Ficus Religiosa*, is the most worthy of notice. It has a woody stem, branching to a great height, with heart-shaped leaves, ending in acute points. Some of the trees are of amazing size, as they are continually increasing, and, contrary to most other things in animal and vegetable life, they appear to be exempt from decay. Every branch from the main body throws out its own roots—at first in small tender fibres several yards from the ground; these continually grow thicker until they reach the surface; and there, striking in, they increase to large trunks, and become parent trees, shooting out new branches from the top; these in time suspend their roots, which, swelling into trunks, produce other branches, and so they continue in a state of progression as long as the earth contributes her sustenance. There are some banian trees in India which actually measure several thousand feet in circumference, and can afford shade and shelter to 8,000 persons.

The Hindoos hold the banian tree in special veneration, often assembling beneath its boughs, like the Druids of old, to perform ceremonies and sacrifices, and not unfrequently placing idols at the foot of the stems in a conspicuous place. The god most generally honoured with this distinction is Ganesha, the sylvan deity, the Pan of the Hindoos, and who is at the same time their Mercury and patron of letters. Rudely carved, he sits in stolid majesty, and receives the homage of his devotees in the shape of red ochre, flowers, grain, and sweetmeats. In form he resembles a short fat man, with "fair round belly," and an elephant's head: he has four hands, one of which holds a shell, another a *chukra* (or quoit), a third a club, and the fourth a water-lily: he sits upon a rat; he has but one projecting tusk, the other having been torn out (so says the mythological tradition) by Vishnu, because Ganesha denied him entrance to the abode of Seva. Ganesha is not only honoured in religious ceremonies, but his protection is invoked by travellers setting out on a journey, and no good Hindoos writes a letter or literary work without commencing with a salutation to Ganesha.

THE PEEPUL (*Ficus Indicus*)—is found in great abundance, and, as some suppose, grows spontaneously; assuredly it rises in most extraordinary places, and often to the great detriment of public buildings, growing out of the cement which connects stones and bricks, and by the violence of its pressure gradually destroying the edifices.

The branches of the young peepul afford a grateful shade, and the growth of the tree is, therefore, encouraged by the natives. It makes its appearance by the sides of the flights of stone steps leading down to *bowlies*, or large wells, above the domes of mosques, through the walls of gardens, &c. No Hindoo dares and no Christian or Mahomedan will condescend to lop off the heads of these young trees, and, if they did, it would only put off the evil and inevitable day, for such are the vital powers of their roots, when they have once penetrated deeply into a building, that they will send out their branches again, cut them off as often as you may, and carry on their internal attack with undiminished vigour. "No wonder," says Colonel Sleeman, "that superstition should have consecrated this tree, delicate and beautiful as it is, to the gods. The palace, the castle, the temple, and the tomb—all those works which man is most proud to raise, to spread, and to perpetuate his name—crumble to dust beneath her withering grasp. She rises triumphant over them all in her lofty beauty, bearing high in air, amidst her light green foliage, fragments of the wreck she has made, to show the nothingness of man's efforts." In the very rudest state of society, among the woods and hills of India, the people have some deity whose power they dread, and whose name they invoke when much is supposed to depend upon the truth of what one man is about to declare. The peepul tree being everywhere sacred to the gods, who are supposed to delight to sit among its leaves and listen to the music of their rustling, the deponent takes one of these leaves in his hand, and invokes the god who sits above him, to crush him, or those dear to him, as he crushes the leaf in his hand, if he speaks anything but the truth: he then plucks and crushes the leaf, and states what he has to say. The large cotton-tree is, among the wild tribes of India, the favourite seat of gods still more terrible, because their superintendence is confined exclusively to the neighbourhood, and having their attention less occupied, they can venture to make a more minute scrutiny into the conduct of the people immediately around them. The peepul is occupied (according to the Hindoos) by one or other of the Hindoo triad, the gods of creation, preservation, and destruction, who have the affairs of the universe to look after, but the cotton and other trees are occupied by some minor deities, who are vested with a local superintendence over the affairs of a district, or perhaps, of a single village.

The Sissoo yields a wood which possesses a very fine grain, and rather handsomely veined. It grows in most of the great forests, intermixed with the *saul;* but in lieu of towering up, with a straight stem, seems partial to crooked forms, such as suit it admirably for the knees of ships, and for such parts as require the grain to follow some particular curve. This wood is extremely hard and heavy, of a dark brown, inclining to a purple tint, when polished; after being properly seasoned, it rarely cracks or warps; nor is it so subject as *saul* to be destroyed by either white ants or river worms. The domestic uses of *sissoo* are chiefly confined to the construction of furniture, especially chairs, tables, tepoys (or tripods), bureaus, bookcases, escritoires, &c., &c., for all which purposes it is peculiarly appropriate, with the exception of its being very ponderous. This objection is, however, counterbalanced by its great durability, and by the extraordinary toughness of the tenons, dovetails, &c., necessarily made by the cabinetmaker or joiner. Sissoo is, of late, more employed than formerly for the frame, ribs, knees, &c., of ships, especially those of great burden; for such it is found to be fully as tough and as durable as the best oak. When timbers can be had of this wood long enough for the purpose, it is often applied for bends, and, indeed, for a portion of the planking or casing; but it is very rarely that a plank of ten feet can be had free from curve.

The SYGWAM, or teak, affords the best timber for building in whatever branch; but its dearness prevents its general use, especially since naval architecture has been so much an object of speculation at Calcutta.

Those who build houses of the first class, rarely fail to build all their terraces upon teak joists; both because they possess superior strength, and that they are far less likely to be attacked by the white ants. This has been attributed to the quantity of *tannin* contained in teak wood, which some have asserted to be a perfect preventive or antidote. There is in teak wood evidently some property, hitherto occult, that repels the white ant, at least for some years, but which is doubtless diminished by exposure to the air, as we find that very old teak timbers became rather more subject to depredation than new ones.

The greater part of the teak used in Bengal and at Madras, is imported from the Pegu coast in immense beams, and in spars, planks, &c., of all sizes. It is by no means unusual to see the squared timbers measuring from forty to fifty feet in length, and averaging from fifteen to twenty inches in diameter.

The TAL-IPOT, or TALPAT tree, is common in the island of Ceylon, and on the coasts of Malabar and Coromandel. It grows very straight and lofty, from eighty to a hundred feet, and has a large tuft of immense leaves at the top. The wood is seldom put to any other use than that of rafters for buildings. Near the root of the tree the wood is black, very hard, and veined with yellow, but the inside is nothing more than pith,—for the sake of which it is sometimes cut down, as the natives make use of it for food, beating it in a mortar till it becomes like flour, when they mix it with water for dough, and bake it. It bears no fruit till the last year of its life. When the flower, which is encased in a sheath (like that of a cocoa-nut), is ripe, the sheath bursts with a loud noise, and emits so disagreeable a smell, that the people sometimes cut it down, not being able to live near it. The fruit is round, and about the size of an apple. It contains two nuts. The most curious and useful part of this tree are its leaves. These hang down from the top, and are nearly circular, and very large—one of them being sufficient to cover fifteen or twenty men. The leaf folds up in plaits, like a fan, and is cut into triangular pieces, which are used everywhere as umbrellas for protection against the sun or rain. The leaf, in strips, is used in schools to teach children to write upon, and as every letter is cut into it by a sharp pointed style, the writing is indelible, and continues legible as long as the leaf itself lasts. The tents of the Kandian kings and others, in time of war, were made of these leaves, and hence were called tal-gé, tal-pat houses. They used to carry with them great quantities of these leaves, already prepared, and cut into proper shape, and thus the labour of erecting a tent was very small. They are also used to cover carts, palankeens, or anything that it is necessary to keep from the sun or rain in travelling.

The COCOA-NUT tree abounds in the peninsula of India, the coast of Burmah, and the west, north, and east parts of the island of Ceylon. It is a tree of immense value to the people and to its possessors.

The tree begins to bear when eight or nine years of age.

Nearly all the domestic wants of the Hindoo and the Cingalese can be supplied by the cocoa-nut tree. He can build his house entirely of it. The walls and doors are made of cadjans (the leaves plaited), the roof is covered with the same, the beams, rafters, &c., are made of the trunk. The builder needs no nails, as he can use the coir rope made from the outside husk.

Works and Pettah of Outtradroog.

If he wants a spout he hollows the trunk, split in two. It also supplies him with spoons, ladles, and cups, pans and drinking vessels, hookah bowls, lamps, and water-buckets; the refuse of the kernel, after the oil is expressed, serves for food for cows and pigs; the milk from the kernel is used in his food. In short, if a man has a few cocoa-nut trees in his garden, he will never starve.

Arrack, a strong spirit, resembling whiskey, is made from toddy, the juice of the flower; and brooms are made from the ribs of the leaflets.

There are many curious customs, traditions, and superstitions, among the Hindoos respecting trees. In planting the mango groves, it is a rule that the trees shall be as far from each other as will prevent their branches from ever meeting. "Plant trees, but let them not touch." Yet the *marriage* of trees is a very common custom. Neither the man who plants a grove nor his wife can taste of the fruit of a mango tree, until he has married one of the trees to some other tree, commonly the tamarind, that grows near it in the same grove. A great deal of pomp and ceremony attends these vegetable unions; and, of course, occasion is taken by the Brahminical priests to make the ceremony one of profit to themselves. The larger the number of Brahmins fed at the marriage, the greater the glory of the proprietor of the grove. Colonel Sleeman relates that, on his visiting the grove of an old man, he asked how many he had feasted; and the man answered, with a sigh, only one hundred and fifty. "He showed me the mango tree which had acted the part of bridegroom on one occasion, but the bride had disappeared from his side. 'And where is the bride, the tamarind?' 'The only tamarind I had in the grove died,' said the old man, 'before we could bring about the wedding; and I was obliged to get a jasmine for a wife for my mango. I planted it here, so that we might, as required, cover both bride and bridegroom under one canopy during the ceremonies; but after the marriage was over the gardener neglected her, and she pined away and died.' 'And what made you prefer the jasmine to all other trees after the tamarind?' 'Because it is the most celebrated of all trees, save the rose.' 'And why not have chosen the rose for a wife?' 'Because no one every heard of a marriage between the rose and the mango; while they take place every day between the mango and the *chumbaelee*, jasmine.'"

In Upper India are many large forest trees, called *kullup*, or *kulpa briksha*, having a soft silvery bark, and scarcely any leaves. It is affirmed and believed by the natives, that the name of the god *Ram*, and his consort *Seeta*, are written by the hand of *God* upon all. Assuredly, Europeans have seen the name of that incarnation of Vishnu written on many *kulpas* in Sanscrit characters, but though there is a softness in the impression, no one is disposed to believe that the writing is supernatural.

In the north-west provinces the people have a curious idea that the shade of the tamarind tree is unwholesome to man and beast, and for this reason they are seldom planted in the groves where caravans are accustomed to halt.

# CHAPTER VIII.

## COMMERCE, COINS, WEIGHTS, MEASURES, &c.

*Articles of export and import—The carrying trade—Exchange—Bullion—The system of weights—The Banyan—Docks—Commercial Office Establishments—The shipping for a twelvemonth.*

IT can hardly be expected that, within the compass of one small volume consecrate to a general account of India, such a description can be given of the commerce of the country, as would satisfy the wishes and expectations of those who may direct their attention to the country with mercantile views. Some thirty years ago or more, Mr. Milburn, an accomplished merchant, deemed the subject of Indian commerce worthy a quarto volume, and since then the establishment of a free trade has opened up so many new sources of wealth and speculation to the enterprising trader, that three such volumes would hardly convey an adequate idea of the resources of the empire, and the extent of its imports and exports.

It would be difficult, in describing the produce of

India, which constitutes her exports, to distinguish very minutely between what has been grown and manufactured within the vast continent, and what has been conveyed thither from the Malayan Peninsula, the islands of the Eastern Archipelago, China, Persia, &c., for the purpose of being reshipped. An enumeration alone can be given of the articles which are brought to England and carried to other lands, leaving to persons interested in such inquiries to distinguish between the absolute offspring of the soil of India, and the goods of which her ports have temporarily become the emporia.

According, then, to the returns, to which access has been obtained, the grand exports from India consist of indigo, sugar, cotton, saltpetre, opium, silk, rice, pepper, betel nuts, coffee, teak timber, tobacco, drugs, dye stuffs, sugar-candy, cocoa-nut oil, cochineal, coir, wax, ginger, cowries (shells), shawls, tamarinds, talc, chillies: all these are undoubtedly the produce of India proper. Of the following very many may be from India, but the most part are yielded by the islands and coasts in her vicinity and the empire of China:—Tea, ivory, lac, gold and silver filigree work, cornelians, ghee, grain, oils, putchock, seeds, soap, horses, sarda, cassia, turmeric, ambergris, colombo root, elephants' teeth, fish maws, sandal wood, zedoary, coarse piece goods, nankeen, dried fruits, tortoise shell, cinnamon, arrack, arica nuts, wild honey, precious stones, copperas, pearls, carpets, dholl, flax, hemp, hides, horns, black salt, copper, tin, lead, wood-oil, earth-oil, dammer, silver, naphtha, birds' nests, timber, rattans, gold dust, camphor, gum benjamin, argus' feathers, kajiput oil, cloves, nutmegs, brimstone, birds of paradise, gum copal, civet, salt, rose water, ottar of roses, sapan wood, tutenague, shrimp caviar, cones, dragons' blood, borax, and a multitude of drugs and cotton piece goods of rude manufacture.

The imports of India comprise every single product of Europe that can be calculated to improve the comfort or promote the luxury of man in a civilized state. The raw cotton received from her is returned, after it has passed through the looms of Manchester, Preston, and Paisley, in millions of yards. Hundreds of ships from England, the Clyde, from France, and the United States, visit her ports annually, laden with hardware and cutlery, with wines, ales, hams, cheeses, woollens, rich glass manufactures, books, bronze articles, steam engines, printing presses, varieties of iron and brass machines, paper, hats, carriages, horses, furniture—in short, every production of nature, every offspring of the handiwork of man, excepting such articles as are only adapted to the severest frosty regions, are carried to India.

The carrying trade between Europe and India is conducted in vessels of all dimensions, from 300 to 1,500 tons. The steamers which ply round the Cape and between the Red Sea of India carry but a small amount of cargo. They are chiefly adapted to the transport of passengers and packets, and only convey a few cases of light goods, books, &c., for which a very heavy freight is demanded. The trade between China and India is carried in ships of considerable burthen, excepting that part of it which concerns the opium grown in India. For this trade, light, fast-sailing clippers are employed. The Malabar coasting trade is borne in large vessels of rude construction, high at the stern and low at the prow, called pattamars and buggalows, the latter of which likewise carry the produce of India to the Arabian and Persian gulfs, and *vice versa*. Along the Coromandel coast to the ports of Calcutta, Arracan, Chittagong, and other places to the eastward, two-masted vessels, denominated dhonies and grabs, are used. The river traffic of India is entrusted to boats of all forms and dimensions, and a great variety of names. On the Ganges a few iron steamers ply, but the cargoes despatched in them rarely consist of anything beyond the supplies of European goods required by the residents and regimental messes in the interior.

The greater part of the transactions between England and India are conducted by bills of exchange, supported by bills of lading of the goods transmitted. The coinage of India consists of rupees, annas, and pice: sixteen annas go to a rupee, and three pysa, or pice, to an anna. The rupee is of silver, about the size of a florin, and is divided into halves and quarters. Sixteen rupees constitute a *gold mohur*, but the continual exportation of bullion and the practice among the natives of melting down gold coins, and converting them into personal ornaments, has caused the total extinction of the coin. It is now merely nominal. In transactions on the coast and with poorer classes of natives, small shells, called cowries, are partially made use of for fractional payments, but their value is subject to continual fluctuations, and they are now nearly superseded by the copper currency.

In the conversion of the rupee into the equivalent currency of other nations in drawing bills of exchange, the fluctuation of the relative value of the precious metals *inter se*, is taken into consideration, from the circumstance of gold being in some, and silver in others, the legal medium of circulation. It is also necessary to take account of the mint charge for coining at each place, which adds a fictitious value to the local coin. The *par of exchange* is, for these reasons, a somewhat ambiguous term, requiring to be distinguished under two more definite denominations. 1st, The *intrinsic par*, which represents that case in which the pure metal contained in the parallel denominations of coins is equal. 2nd, The *commercial par*, or that case in which the current value of the coin at each place (after deducting the seignorage leviable for coinage) is equal; or, in other words, "two sums of money of different countries are *commercially* at par, while they can *purchase* an equal quantity of the same kind of pure metal."

Thus, if silver be taken from India to England, it must be sold to a bullion merchant at the market price, the proprietor receiving payment in gold (or notes convertible into it). The London mint is closed against the importer of silver, which metal has not, therefore, a minimum value in the English market, fixed by the mint price, although it has so in Calcutta, where it may always be converted into coin at a charge of two per cent. On the other hand, if a remittance in gold be made from India to England, its out-turn there is known and fixed. The new Calcutta *gold mohur* fluctuates as considerably in India as that of silver does in England; the natural tendency of commerce being to bring to an equilibrium the operations of exchange in the two metals.

The exchange between England and India has, therefore, a twofold expression; for silver, the price of the sicca rupee in shillings and pence; for gold, the price of the sovereign in rupees.

The system of British India weights and measures is founded upon the principle of making the *maund*, or highest nominal weight, equal to one hundred English troy pounds; and thirty-five *seers* equal to seventy-two pounds avoirdupois, thus establishing a simple connection, void of fractions, between the two English metrical scales and that of India. The unit of the British India ponderary system is called the *tola*. It weighs 180 grains, English troy weight. From it upwards are derived the heavy weights, viz., the *chittack*, the *seer*, and *maund*:—

| | | lbs. | oz. | dwts. | grs. | |
|---|---|---|---|---|---|---|
| The maund is equal to | . . . | 100 | 0 | 0 | 0 | troy. |
| The seer ,, | . . . | 2 | 6 | 0 | 0 | ,, |
| The chittack ,, | . . . | 1 | 17 | 12 | 0 | ,, |
| The tola ,, | . . . | 0 | 0 | 7 | 12 | ,, |

Goldsmiths and jewellers use smaller weights, such as the *masha*, *ruttee*, and *dhan*. One *masha* is equivalent to fifteen grains, and one *ruttee* to 1·875. The *dhan* only weighs one quarter of a grain.

In the straits of Malacca and Manilla, and in the island of Ceylon, the Spanish dollar forms the chief currency: but English money and rupees are nevertheless a legal tender, the rupee being valued at 1*s*. 11*d*.

Bank-notes issued by the banks of India, are current throughout the country, but they form comparatively a small part of the circulation. Bills of exchange, called *hoondees*, are employed as a means of remittance from one part of the country to another, and are obtained from the bankers and shroffs, who are found scattered all over the country. The rest of the paper-money consists of Treasury notes, bills issued by the civil officers of Government for equivalent, to facilitate the remittable operations of their own servants and others. The most secure investment of savings is in the Government paper, or promissory notes which are issued, bearing interest at four or five per cent. per annum according to the necessity of the Government, and the state of the money-market at the moment of opening a loan. All trust property, all the estates of intestate persons, are required to be converted into Government paper. It is the only security recognised by the authorities, and any amount of money can be obtained, at a reasonable interest, on the deposit of such paper (which may be compared to English Exchequer bills) when parties are not inclined to sell out their stock.

A considerable portion of the capital employed in the India trade, is supplied by English merchants. They depute members of their firms, or confidential clerks, to proceed to the Presidencies to establish commercial houses, and there to purchase and transmit produce to England, China, Australia, and the East Indian Archipelago, and to obtain a market for English produce and manufactures. These gentlemen are assisted in duties so new to them by a class of natives called Banyans.

The term BANYAN implies a Hindoo merchant, shopkeeper, or confidential cashier and broker. The term is used in Bengal to designate the native who manages the money concerns of the European, and sometimes serves him as an interpreter.

At Madras the same description of person is called a *dubash*, a corruption of *dwi bashi*, one who can speak two languages. Some banyans usurp the designation of *dewan*, which should imply an extensive delegated power; that office, under the Emperors of Hindostan, and even now in the courts of Lucknow, Hyderabad, &c., being confidential, and never bestowed but on persons in high favour. The banyans are invariably Hindoos, possessing, in general, very large property, with most extensive credit and influence. So much is this the case that Calcutta was, some years ago, absolutely under the control of about twenty or thirty banyans, who managed every concern in which they could find means to make a profit. It is inconceivable what property was in their hands. They were the ostensible agents in every line of business, placing their dependents in the several departments over which themselves had obtained dominion. If a contract was to be made with Government by any gentlemen not in the Company's service, the banyans became the securities, under the condition of receiving a per-centage, and of appointing their friends to such duties as might control the principal and save themselves from loss. When a person in the service of the Company was desirous of deriving benefit from some contract, in the disposal of which he had a vote, and which, consequently, he could not obtain in his own name, then the banyan became the principal, and the donor either received a share or derived advantage from loans, &c., answering his purpose equally well. The same person frequently was banyan to several European gentlemen, all of whose concerns were, of course, accurately known to him, and thus became the subject of conversation at those meetings the banyans of Calcutta invariably held, and do yet hold, after the active business of the day has been adjusted.

A banyan invariably goes attended by several underling *sircars*, *hircarahs*, &c. He, to a certain degree, rules the office; entering it generally with little ceremony, making a slight obeisance, and never divesting himself of his slippers—a privilege which, in the eyes of the natives, at once places him on a footing of equality with his employers. Of late years, however, the power of the banyan has dimininished greatly; for, if we except a few large concerns, such as banking houses, and the principal merchants, who, having valuable cargoes on hand, are each under the necessity of retaining one of these people, for the purpose of obtaining cash to make up payments, or to furnish advances to indigo factors, &c., no one troubles himself with a banyan. It cannot, however, be denied that many speculations are carried on by the aid of *banyans*, which, but for the strength of their resources, could never have been attempted. We owe our present extended trade in the fabrics of Dacca, &c.; in the sugar of the western and northern districts; in indigo throughout the country, and numerous other branches of commerce, to the support given by this class to such gentlemen as appeared to them likely to succeed.

All the produce of the world which reaches India is deposited in extensive warehouses called *godowns*, or in bonded warehouses. The cotton, which is brought from the interior of the country, is carried to lofty buildings where ponderous screws are established, and is there screwed into bales of a compact form, previous to its shipment. At two of the Presidencies, Calcutta and Bombay, are dockyards. Those at Bombay are wet docks, where some of the finest British men-of-war have been constructed of the teak of the Malabar or Tenasserim coasts, each vessel often bringing home a duplicate of herself in the form of cargo, to be put together on her arrival in England.

Every mercantile house in India has an establishment of clerks, chiefly natives, who write English correctly, and keep accounts upon the English system with surprising accuracy. The salaries of the clerks (*baboos* and *sircars*, *keranies* and *purvoes*, as they are called at the several Presidencies) are much lower than they are in this country, the highest salary rarely exceeding 15*l.* per mensem, and the great majority averaging 3*l.* to 5*l.* per month. Attached to the offices of business also are a number of peons or sepoys, to run upon errands, and convey *chits* or notes, of which the circulation is immense in a country where Europeans cannot move about much, and have no recognised Exchanges or other places of rendezvous.

We cannot close this chapter without submitting a statement of the amount of shipping which has sailed to and from India during the past twelvemonth. It will afford some idea of the extent of the trade carried on between the limits of the East India Company's charter :—

| From | To London. | To Liverpool. | To Bristol and Hull. | To the Clyde. | Total. |
|---|---|---|---|---|---|
| Calcutta . . . . | 195 | 85 | 5 | 8 | 293 |
| Madras . . . . . . | 46 | 7 | 0 | 0 | 53 |
| Bombay . . . . . . | 31 | 48 | 4 | 8 | 91 |
| China . . . . . . | 87 | 27 | 0 | 3 | 117 |
| Ceylon . . . . . . | 53 | 0 | 0 | 0 | 53 |
| Singapore and Penang | 27 | 11 | 0 | 1 | 39 |
| Phillipine Islands . | 7 | 2 | 0 | 0 | 9 |
| Java and Sumatra . | 10 | 0 | 0 | 0 | 10 |
| Arabia . . . . . . | 2 | 0 | 0 | 0 | 2 |
| New South Wales, New Zealand, &c. | 133 | 6 | 0 | 1 | 140 |
| Mauritius . . . . | 71 | 15 | 20 | 25 | 131 |
| Cape of Good Hope . | 37 | 2 | 1 | 0 | 40 |

This is an increase of forty vessels over the preceding year. The increase in the number of vessels which cleared *outwards* is still greater. It amounts to 155 vessels, comprising a tonnage of 129,375 tons, and within the quarter ending 31st March, there has been an increase of 181 outward, and 58 inward vessels. The return of vessels does not include the steamers, of which some thirty or forty reach India with light goods and small packages, in the course of the year.

# CHAPTER IX.

## THE FRUITS OF INDIA.

*The Pine-apple—The Custard-apple—The Mango—The Egg-plum—The Pomegranate—The Melon—The Guava—The Plantain—The Pumplenose—The Papaya—The Loquat—The Jack—The Leechee, &c.*

NATURE, as if anticipating the abstinence of millions of Hindoos from the use of animal food, has been wonderfully liberal of her supply of vegetable diet. No part of the world is so fruitful of those products, which are at once nutritious and agreeable. Every fruit and vegetable known to mild, and even cold regions, is produced on the hills or the plains of India; and in addition to these, vast varieties, peculiar to the tropics, grow in luxurious abundance. To enumerate them all would be impossible, within the limits of this volume, and the quality of many would be difficult of description without the aid of the horticulturist and the naturalist. Let it suffice, that the fertile soil of India yields mangoes, pine-apples, plantains, pomegranates, pumplenoses, jacks, custard-apples, leechees, guavas, melons, oranges, lemons, limes, grapes, sour sops, almonds, gooseberries, strawberries, tamarinds, plums, figs, dates, citrons, loquats, potatoes, cabbages, cucumbers, yams, brinjalls, peas, beans, artichokes, salads, celery, beetroot, cauliflower, nollcoll, mangosteens, &c., &c., most of which, at some time or other, are found upon the tables of Europeans.

THE PINE-APPLE (*bromelia ananas*) is called by the natives *anarush*. As the name of the fruit is Persian, and there being no Sanscrit one, it is supposed to be an imported fruit in India, though common all over the country, where the climate is not too severe for its growth in the open air; a green-house, hot-house, or *cool*-house for plants or fruits, being yet entirely unknown in India, even amongst Europeans. The common bazaar pine of India is a very inferior fruit to the English hot-house pine, and even to those which have been raised with care and under shade (which they seem to prefer), in India. Those of the eastern islands are very far superior, the commonest Malay, or Javanese anana being equal, it is said, to the best in India,—except, perhaps, those of Goa and other Portuguese establishments on the western coast, where, as in the case of the mango and some other fruits, we still find traces of the care which the early Portuguese colonists bestowed on them. This is probably owing to peculiarities of soil and climate, as well as care; though the Portuguese, like the Dutch, were good gardeners, and paid attention to horticulture, which the English, hitherto, cannot be said to have done. It is said, and with much justice, that no fruit in India requires to be eaten more cautiously than this, both by new comers and new residents. It is accused, and with some considerable truth, of occasioning very severe and dangerous attacks of pseudo-cholera and dysentery. To the newly arrived Europeans, especially of the lower orders, it is indeed a tempting fruit, and its powerful acid and tough flesh may often make it dangerous to them. An exceedingly beautiful flax, of great fineness and strength, may be prepared from the leaves of this plant by simple maceration and beating. In the Philippine Islands, dresses equal to the finest muslin are woven from it, and embroidered with extraordinary taste; and though expensive, they last for many years, being in duration, colour, and beauty, equal to fine Flanders lace.

THE INDIAN CUSTARD-APPLE (*annona squamosa*) is called by the natives, *ata*, the fruit of a small tree which grows about fifteen feet high in all parts of India. The leaves are smooth and soft, and about three inches long, tapering at both ends. The fruit is nearly round, with a rough outside, about the size of an orange. When ripe, it is easily burst. It is filled with a soft white substance, of a sweet taste, and separable into small portions, each containing a small black seed. It bears once a-year. The fruits are ripe in July, and are much sought after. Perhaps there is no Indian fruit about which we hear so many various opinions expressed by Europeans. To some it is the most delicious fruit in the country, while to others its flavour seems not merely a mawkish sweetness, but almost nauseating. In a word, it is rare to meet two persons who agree in their opinion of the custard-apple. Care should be taken when eating it not to scrape off with the spoon the part which adheres to the outside scales of the fruit; for this certainly will, if frequently repeated, cause a smart inflammatory sore throat; and the finer the fruit the more liable it is to cause this. The part which surrounds the seeds, and which adheres to them, should alone be eaten. The kernels of the seeds are also poisonous, though the seeds are frequently swallowed whole without any ill effects. In countries where it meets with peculiar soils and careful cultivation, as in the Mauritius and the Eastern islands, the ata attains a very large size, at least double that of the largest in India, and its flavour is generally improved; this last difference may be observed here, and indeed with many fruits in all countries; the largest sized are generally the best flavoured. There is much uncertainty as to whence this fruit, and its congener, the *annona reticulata*, or sour-sop of the West Indies, were originally derived; it has been supposed that both were brought from Spanish or Portuguese America, and thus propagated through their Asiatic dominions, and to China; though, from its abundance in China and Cochin China, it may equally have been obtained from those countries. It is probable that the Portuguese settlements on the eastern coast of Africa may have furnished it on the one side and China on the other; but if the truth be told, there is but little or nothing known of what are the peculiarities of the various kinds of this and many other fruits, which are, however, well worthy of more attention and study than they have hitherto obtained from us. The *annona reticulata* is said to be indigenous in the mountainous country of South America, and the absence of any Sanscrit name for the fruit is evidence enough that it is of foreign introduction, though now the commonest fruit in India.

THE MANGO (fruit of the *mangifera Indica*), or as the natives call it, *aum*, is a rich fruit, of a bright orange-coloured pulp, and a coat of orange or green, intermingled with a red bloom. There are in India so many sorts and varieties of this rich fruit, which, in fact, may be called, from its abundance, the Indian apple, that it would take a volume to describe them. As a mere tree it is valuable, being of not very slow growth, and affording by its dense, dark shade, the most grateful shelter from "the traveller's enemy"—the sun. Its wood is most extensively used, and, in fact, the planks supply, for a large part of India, the uses of fir plank in Europe, and when carefully preserved by paint, it lasts many years. The fruits, in their season, are so abundant in all the bazaars that the cows are often regaled with them, and always with the stones, which they crunch, apparently with great delight. A curious fact is, that in remote villages, near extensive forest tracks, the bears, at the season of the fruit, are known to invade the mango *topes*, and to take possession of them till they have devoured all the fruit, in spite of all the efforts of the villagers to drive them out! The finest mangoes on the Bengal side of India are said to be those of Malda; though there are certainly some in the neighbourhood of Calcutta equal, or superior to them. The finest in all India are said to be those of Goa, where they have been cultivated by the Portuguese. Until of late years, however, little or no attention was paid to the sorts planted, or, at all events, it was rarely thought, by the natives at least, worth the trouble or expense of sending for good kinds; the *topes*, indeed, being as often planted as an act of piety, to afford shade, as for the fruit, which he who planted rarely expected to taste. Good grafts, and these upon good stocks, are now more sought after, especially in the neighbourhood of large towns, where a few mango trees, if bearing choice fruit, are valuable property. Perhaps nothing can show more strongly what the mango may become by careful cultivation, than the fact, that at the plantation of Black River, in the Isle of France, no less than twelve varieties, of the most exquisite flavour, of sizes from a large apple to that of a man's head, some almost without stones, have been obtained by the care and attention of a long series of years. The mango in India is eaten in every possible form; and an extensive trade is carried on in the young green and acid fruits, which, being dried in the sun, are sold in all the bazaars as a favourite condiment for curries. The crop of this fruit is very uncertain, as the prevalence of fogs at the time of flowering, drought, or storms, will often destroy a large crop in a few hours.

THE EGG-PLUM (*ziziphus jujuba*) is called by the natives, *bair*. Of this fruit there are several varieties. Originally from Western India and Persia, it is now naturalized in all the gardens about Calcutta, and in some of the larger towns. The inferior and hedge sorts are met with all over India. The common wild kind much resembles in shape, colour, flavour, and size, an unripe crab-apple, and one would almost suppose that from it a good cider might be made. The better and fine sorts are of the flavour of an inferior apple, or wild plum. They are eaten in large quantities by natives of India, by whom the fruit, in all its states, is very highly esteemed, not only when green and ripe, but also when dried and preserved in various ways. The best produce of the wild tree, however, is not its fruit, but the strong and durable silk (*tusser*) which it produces. The trees, even in the midst of the towns, are often seen with numbers of worms upon them; and in the districts where the silk is an object of culture, the moths are bred from the cocoons, and the worms fed upon the leaves like silk-worms. They are, however, kept in close baskets, being very active, and crawling away fast, if left on open spots. The great enemies to the culture are crows and other birds, and ants, which devour the young caterpillars in all the stages of their growth.

POMEGRANATE (*Punica granatum*), the Hindostanee word for which is *dalim*. From Spain to Persia, and from Persia to China, the pomegranate is held in high repute, not only as a delicious, cooling, and highly wholesome fruit, but as a remedy, a principal ingredient in many drinks, sherbets, and sweetmeats; and, finally, as a source of allusions for lovers, poets, warriors, and orators. In inter-tropical India, except at considerable elevations, it is rarely found of a fine quality, being mostly not of the sweet kind, but of the sour, becoming even stringent as the fruit approaches more to the common wild kind. It is an object of much care and attention in the south of Europe and Barbary, both as a fruit, as a flowering plant, and as one proper for garden hedges and covering of walls in espaliers, or something between the espalier and the creeper. This it is to a very considerable height and extent, its numerous branches forming a close covering, and its brilliant flowers and excellent fruit making it an object of great beauty, and even of value in some situations, where the flowers and fruit are all saleable to the druggists or the dyers. The bark of its root is also, there is no doubt, an invaluable remedy against that frightfully severe disease, the tape-worm, which, before the knowledge of it, had baffled, both in India and Europe, all the skill of physicians.

THE MELON, or *foonti*.—Of melons there are many varieties in India, but there are few of the Bengal sorts worth eating; for their flavour, except in the northern or north-western provinces, where the Persian and Affghan conquerors have brought some good kinds, is very indifferent. In inter-tropical India the best melons almost immediately degenerate into a sort of half water-melon. A few successful attempts have been made, with great care and attention, to raise fine high-flavoured melons from seed obtained from England, France, and Affghanistan; but it is yet only by a succession of fresh seed that good ones can be obtained, and the care and cost are such, that hitherto there seems little chance of counting the melon of Persia, Affghanistan, or Europe amongst the Indian fruits. The water-melon in some parts of India attains to a monstrous size. Those of Agra, which are cultivated on the sandy flats left by the subsiding waters of the

Jumna, are famous; and stories of them are standard jokes of approved currency in those parts. On the coast they are also considered to attain "great respectability;" and, in short, good water-melons are pretty common all over India, and they are very highly esteemed by the natives and by many Europeans. The foonti, or phootee, as it is called by the Bengalees, has a strong melon scent, but very little of the taste, and less of the perfume of the true melon. To some Europeans, and to most natives, however, it is an acceptable fruit, at least as a change, during the short time that it is in season, and in great demand for the various preparations, such as sherbets, and the like, into which it enters. It is like all the tribe, considered as cooling, and even medicinal, and no doubt justly so.

THE GUAVA, called in Hindustani, *soopri am*, is a fruit of the *psidium pomiferum* and *pyriferum*. The fruit is usually thought to be originally from the West Indies, but it is certain that there is more than one African, and several Chinese and Cochin-Chinese species or varieties, both of the edible and wild sorts. These may, it is true, have been carried to China by the early voyagers, and India may have received hers from the coasts of Africa, with which, long before Europeans visited her shores, she held a steady intercourse. The most remarkable evidence of its being of foreign introduction in India, is that it has, we believe, no Sanscrit name. Thence we suppose it, like tobacco, to have been brought, perhaps about the same time. The facility with which this fruit is propagated from its numerous fertile seeds, of which the hard shell resists insects and the other destructive influences for a very long period, renders it one of the most common in India. The strong flavour of the common sorts is usually found disagreeable to newly arrived Europeans, but to this custom reconciles; and the finer sorts, of which one, the *psidium microphylla*, or true West Indian sort, has the flavour of the raspberry; and another, a large and very rich kind, has scarcely any of the strong taste of the bazaar guavas. There are some very fine varieties amongst the Malay Islands; for with the Malays and Chinese, as with the natives of India, this, like all high-flavoured fruits, is a favourite. By Europeans it is more generally eaten and stewed in wine, and for the well known jelly made from it, when much of its flavour disappears. The leaves of the tree are somewhat aromatic, and much used in the Eastern Islands medicinally, or as a substitute for the betel-leaf. The wood of the old trees is exceeding close-grained and tough, and in some degree resembles boxwood. It is much used amongst the natives of India for gun-stocks, as it takes a good polish, and is rarely known to split with heat, or fracture from blows.

THE PLANTAIN (*musa paradisiaca*), called by the natives *kela*. The varieties of the plantain in India are innumerable both as to size and taste. With respect to size, there are the diminutive *chumpa*, which might be clasped by "an alderman's thumb-ring," and the great Dacca plantain, which is nine or ten inches long, and proportionably thick. Indian plantains, however, are but dwarfs compared to the great Madagascar ones, which are as large as a man's forearm; and those, even, are small, compared to a sort produced in the mountains of the Phillipine Islands, of which a single fruit is said to be a load for a man! As to quality, there are some of the wild kinds, which, says Roxburgh, are "not even fit for a monkey to eat," and others, of the cultivated sorts, of which the flavour approaches to that of the richest pear. Some also, and those are in great demand amongst the natives, require, like potatoes, to be boiled, or roasted on the embers, before they are eatable, though many of them become excellent. Of this kind are all the monstrous sorts spoken of above. The plantains and bananas are not merely fruit, they are also a very considerable article of food amongst the natives of all the nations of the East, as well as of the West, who possess this invaluable fruit, and most of the sorts are very wholesome. The uses of the wild plantain are, as yet, not fully known in India. Valuable cordage is made from the stems in large quantities and extensively exported from Manilla to all parts of the world; of this manufacture, the natives in India are wholly ignorant, and it is singular, that abounding as the forests in some parts are with wild kinds, no European has yet shown them that the fibres give a valuable hemp, or indeed both hemp and the finest flax; for, not only are the largest cables made from it, but also tissues almost as fine as those from fibres of the anana. The fruit from the plantain, when dried in the sun, is found to keep perfectly for a length of time, and to resemble a rich fig. The plaintain leaf is of great utility. It forms plates and dishes for the natives, and the cool upper side is constantly applied by our medical men in India, as dressings for blisters, or as a covering for the shaven head, in cases of brain fever.

THE PUMPLENOSE (*citrus decumanus*).—There seems no doubt with botanists that Java is the native country of this fine fruit, of which the best varieties almost rival a good orange, and its easy growth and abundant bearing make it in fact pretty nearly the orange of the inter-tropical country, or where, from want of elevation or peculiarity of soil or climate, the orange is difficult to rear. This is the case in Calcutta, which is supplied with oranges from the Sylhet Hills. In the West Indies, this fruit is called the shaddock, and is said to be so named after the captain of the ship who brought it from the East, which seems probable, for it is not mentioned in the writings of the early Spanish authors. The varieties of the fruit are numerous, and of all degrees of flavour, from that of a rich sugary orange, melting in the mouth, to a tough, half-sour, and half-dry taste, which prejudices many against the fruit. It is a singularity, that the trees which bear very fine ones one year, will give but indifferent ones the next; but this may be owing to the utter want of all care and culture, which our tree fruits invariably experience. A tree which gives fruit is, to the native of Bengal, something so ready-made to his hand, that he does not seem even to suspect it can be improved. In Upper India, where, through their Tartar, Persian, and Affghan neighbours and conquerors, they have some ideas of gardening, and even books upon it, much more attention is paid to these matters; but the climate there becomes too severe for the pumplenose. There can be no doubt, from the richness of flavour of the finer sorts, that they are susceptible of vast improvement. The sherbet prepared from them is a most grateful drink to the sick; and the fruit itself, if good ones can be had, is an invaluable sea stock.

THE PAPAYA (*carica papaya*).—This fruit, though abounding in India, is a well recognised importation from the West Indies or Africa, where it is found abundantly, and of far larger size than those of the common Indian growth. As a fruit, eaten both raw and boiled, pickled or preserved, it ranks high; the choice ones being of a very rich and somewhat melon-like flavour when eaten with sugar and wine. As a tree, it is highly ornamental; few garden or orchard trees surpass it in gracefulness of appearance, in which indeed it approaches to the palm. The size and beauty of the leaf, and even of the leaf-stalks, are always much admired when closely examined by those to whom the wonders of tropical vegetation are new. One of the curious properties of the papaya-tree is, that it renders tough or newly-killed meat, tender, when hung up amongst its leaves for a few hours, which effect is also produced by some other trees.

THE LOQUAT (*mespilus japonica*).—As a pretty and almost a picturesque fruit and tree, the loquat may rank very high, for the dark-green foliage of the tree, and twice in the year, the rich perfume of the flower, which renders it a great addition to the garden and equally so to the dessert, when served with a few of their leaves. Of the properties of the fruit there is but little to say, being almost what the French would call *un fruit insignifiant* in India, though much prized in its native countries of China and Japan, where it grows to a much larger size, and has a far richer flavour than in India, or even in the Eastern Islands, in all of which countries the climate seems too warm and moist for it; while in Northern India, though it may there have the winter which it evidently requires, it has not the same degree of moisture; the winter of China and Japan being, as compared with those of India, wet winters. Amongst the natives of India it does not seem to be a fruit much thought of or prized, not being common in their gardens at any distance from large towns, and probably not being sufficiently high-flavoured. Amongst the Europeans there also it is nearly neglected, and when it appears, may be said to be rather tasted as a novelty than eaten as a favourite fruit. Amongst the Chinese and Dutch in the Eastern Islands, it is, however, much more prized, and the culture of the tree much attended to. Presents of fine sorts are frequently interchanged, and from the gardens of some of the wealthy Chinese, and Malay-Chinese, Portuguese, and Dutch families of the olden times, who are all capital horticulturists, and have, in the great Chinese population of those countries, excellent gardeners, the fruit is really a delicious one.

THE JACK, which in shape and size is not unlike a *horse's head,* grows undeniably out of the body of the tree. It has an exceedingly rough, green outside, thickly covered with short blunted prickles. When cut open it is full of kernels, or seeds, about the size of a small plumb, each of which is imbedded in yellow pulp, which, through disagreeable in smell, is by no means so in taste, being full of saccharine matter. It is much eaten by the natives in this state, as well as used in curries. When the fruit is cut from the tree, a thick, milky gum in large quantities drops from it. The kernels are often boiled and used at table as vegetables; the taste is like that of beans. The general size of the jack fruit is about one foot nine inches long, and two feet six inches round. Some are much larger; it is often the case that one is as much as a person can carry.

LEECHEE (*neechee phol*) is a purely Chinese fruit, for it bears no other name but its Chinese one in any part of the world. Like most foreign fruits, it has much degenerated in India, from the utter want of culture, and by propagation from seed only; the natives, except a few gardeners about the large towns, being wholly ignorant of grafting, and too indifferent to practise it, or to give a young plant the care and attention necessary to produce a fine fruit-bearing tree. Hence, with the exception of some from the Botanic Gardens, Calcutta, the majority of the leechees in India are of a most inferior description, and not to be compared with those of China, Batavia, the Mauritius, and Bourbon. It is, moreover, in and about Calcutta, a very capricious fruit-tree as to its bearings, the crop being very subject to failure from various causes; and even when the fruit is ripening, the trees must be covered with netting, to prevent the fruit being destroyed by the rapacious crows, which, with the squirrels, are the great enemies of all fruit gardening in Lower India, as the monkeys are in other parts. While the leechee lasts, however—and its duration is but for about a month in any perfection—it is a rich addition to the dessert, and to the breakfast-table. The Chinese dry it in ovens, and in the sun, and it is thus exported in considerable quantities; but in this state it is little sought after in India. The juice of the fruit is perfectly wholesome. In countries where the leechee abounds, and from its sweetness and rich flavour it is greedily eaten by children, deaths from indigestion and obstructions brought on by this cause are so common, when the fruit is in season, that in slave colonies the fruit is often broken from the trees when green, to avoid this danger to the children and the young negroes. The leechee-tree is very hardy, and will bear cold, heat, excessive rains, and even inundation for weeks, without apparent suffering, though doubtless the fruit is affected in quantity or quality by these trials.

THE NOONA (*annona reticulata*), the sour sop, is a very ordinary fruit in the East; those of the West Indies have a superior flavour. The fruit is eaten both raw and roasted in embers; its bark, or hard external skin is a powerful astringent and tonic, and of great use in native medicine, particularly amongst the Malays and Chinese, who also use it in some of their dyeing processes. The tree does not grow to a size which would allow the wood to be of any use. The fruit is much coveted by bats, squirrels, monkeys, and other vermin, which in the East so completely disappoint the hopes of the gardener.

THE JAMROOL (*eugenia alla* or *aquea*), is a tasteless white fruit. This tree is mostly planted for ornament, its bright, pale, and almost transparent fruit, hanging in clusters amongst the large, dark green leaves, rendering it an object of pecular beauty. The Malays and natives of India, who are great lovers of watery fruits, which they eat as cooling medicines, think very highly of the jamrool, and eat it in large quantities during its season, which is always the hottest month of the year. The Malay name for it is a very expressive one, *jamber arger* (the water *jamba*), and, with them the bark is thought a sovereign remedy for apthæ in children. The fruits of all the family appear to be singularly attractive to bats of all kinds and sizes, which swarm about the trees at the time of its ripening; the large bats will even cut through a net to get at the fruit, and are thus caught by those tribes of Coolies, Dangurs, and Boornwaks, who esteem a dish of stewed bats as a delicacy, and sometimes pass a night in hunting them, with as much perseverance and zest as the English sportsmen follows the snipe or the floriken.

# CHAPTER X.

## THE CLIMATE OF INDIA.

*General range of the thermometer—Bengal, Madras, and Bombay—Remedies for heat—Diseases of India—Hill stations.*

"How about the climate?" is a question which very naturally suggests itself to all persons purposing to take up their abode in India. Any advantages in the shape of pecuniary gain and social position which India may confer are dearly purchased at the expense of health; indeed, these advantages cannot be reaped at all if there is not some measure of certainty, or some reasonable chance, that the climate will be found suited to the constitutions of those who may proceed to either of the Presidencies.

Of course, in so vast a continent, varied in its physical features, and embracing twenty degrees of latitude, there must necessarily be a great diversity of climate. The air of the hills is purer and cooler than that of the plains; the presence of jungle and swamp is more pernicious than their absence; excessive aridity is as injurious as superabundant moisture. In India we find all the topographical peculiarities which induce

Hill Fortress.

contrariety of effect; and each Presidency is more or less affected by its difference of geographical position.

The situation of Bengal is low and level: in some parts remarkable for a dry and sandy—in others for a moist and clayey—soil. For eight months in the year, that is, from November to June, scarcely a drop of rain falls, excepting in the shape of an occasional storm, which lays the dust and cools the heated atmosphere. On the other hand, from July to October inclusive, a dry day is a rarity. Rain either falls for many days together, or for certain portions of each day, swelling the rivers and the tanks and diffusing universal humidity. To enable the reader to judge of the degree of heat, without reference to qualifying circumstances, it will suffice to state that the lowest range of the thermometer in January is 52° early in the morning, and its highest 65° in the afternoon. This is mild and pleasant enough. At no period of the year does the thermometer fall below 52°. After January it gradually begins to ascend, reaching in the evening of February 75°; in the afternoon of March 82°. In April the mercury runs up to 90° in the shade and 110° in the sun. In May it ranges in the shade from 85° in the morning to 93° in the afternoon, rising to 140° if exposed to the sun. June finds it still on the ascent. It is frequently 99° in the shade at noon; but the rains begin to fall in the middle of the month, and the air becomes cooler as we advance towards July. The thermometer, in the latter month, falls to 80° and 89°. It preserves the same range in August. In September it falls to 78° in the morning, going up to 85° in the afternoon. In October it seldom reaches a higher range than 80° in the afternoon, whence it declines in November to 75°, and in December to 65° in the afternoon.

The seasons at Bombay correspond with those of

Calcutta. The thermometer takes much the same range as in Bengal; and although, in the hottest months, the casual advantage of a thunder-storm is never obtained, the sea breezes which set in towards the middle of the day essentially mitigate the heat of the atmosphere. Early in June the S. W. monsoon commences, the rains fall in rich abundance, and the air becomes cool and agreeable.

The Madras seasons and temperature differ from those of the other Presidencies. January and February are the coldest months of the year. The thermometer ranges between 75° and 78°. Rain falls in slight showers continually, leaving a deposit of fractions of an inch. From March to June the range is between 76° and 87°. In July the rains commence, and the thermometer then falls to 84°. It retains that position with very little deviation through August, and about four inches of rain fall. In September the thermometer falls to 83°, and the rain increases. In October the clouds begin to assume a more dense appearance than heretofore; the thermometer declines to an average of 81°, and the rainy season fairly commences, just as it has terminated at the other Presidencies. During November the rains fall very heavily—not less than fourteen inches being deposited. The thermometer falls to 75° in December, and the rains abate.

Of course, every scheme that human ingenuity can devise to mitigate the discomfort of heat is resorted to. The punkah is continually kept swinging over the head of the European; the window-blinds of the houses are closed to exclude as much light as may be consistent with convenience; matting of fragrant grass is placed at doors and windows, and continually watered; and every possible attention is paid by the prudent to clothing and to diet. From November to March woollen clothes may be worn with advantage: during the rest of the year everybody is clad in white cotton. No one ventures into the sun without parasols of a broad and shady form, or in palankeens roofed with tuskas.

Nevertheless the European constitution is exposed to the attacks of many diseases. Fevers, dysentery, affections of the liver, cholera morbus, and rheumatism, are common; and there are numerous minor disorders, the effect of climate acting upon a slight or an excessively robust system, which few can escape. These latter consist of a troublesome cutaneous eruption called prickly heat, boils, and ulcers. Boils grow to a large size, are excessively painful and disturbing, and the lancet is often necessary to the relief of the patient. Constipation is also a common complaint, needing exercise and stimulating medicines.

Yet it does not follow that all persons should be assailed by the diseases of India. Very many individuals go through life in all parts of the empire, with perhaps only a single attack of one or two of the greater complaints—and not a few will pass thirty years in India unscathed. The writer of these pages was singularly favoured. During a residence of twenty-one years—one half the time at Bombay, and the other half at Calcutta—he never had a single day's illness.

And if sickness should overtake the dwellers in any one of the Presidencies, baffling the skill of the practitioner, great facilities exist for resorting to the sanatory hills in the vicinity of each town. The resident of Calcutta can find relief by proceeding to the Darjeling mountain—one of the Sinchul range—where he finds a climate as temperate as that of his own native land. The place is reached by very easy stages in three or four days, and from the burning plain the invalid finds himself transported 7,200 feet above the level of the sea in a temperature of 55°. From Madras the Neilgherry hills are reached with ease in a week, and at Ootacumand, the principal station, or settlement, the finest climate in the world is found, and convalescence rapidly achieved. Bombay boasts its Mahabuleshwar hills, which are less than seventy miles distant, and easily accessible by boat or palankeen. Here the mean annual temperature is at 66°, and beautiful scenery, added to healthful breezes, gives life to the valetudinarian.

# CHAPTER XI.

## THE WILD SPORTS OF INDIA.

*Jackall hunting—Boar hunting—Tiger hunting—The man tiger—The Nepaul Terai—Elephant hunting—Bear hunting—Deer stalking.*

THE axe and the plough have been at work during the past fifty years to reclaim the jungle, the forest, and the wastes of India; and the sporting ardour of the European Nimrods has dealt deadly havoc among the animals which found shelter and sustenance in these wilds and wildernesses; but, nevertheless, a large quantity of land is still monopolized by untamed and untameable quadrupeds and feathered game of infinite varieties; and in the pursuit of them the English residents of the Mofussil (or interior) find abundant sources of excitement and entertainment.

The animals which chiefly abound in India, are the tiger, the leopard, the bear, the elephant, the lion, the wolf, the boar, the jackall, the buffalo, the hyena, the jaguar, the jungle cat, the wild dog, the lynx, and many varieties of deer, from the *sambur* of the hills to the antelope of the plains. Among the feathered tribe are the floriken, pheasants (white and golden), partridges, bustards, pea fowl, jungle cocks and hens (smaller than, but resembling in plumage, the domestic fowl), quails, pigeons, wild ducks, teal, wild geese, snipe, ortolans, plovers, &c.

Excepting jackall-hunting and snipe-shooting, very little field sport is to be enjoyed in the immediate neighbourhood of the Presidency towns of Calcutta, Madras, and Bombay. It is the exclusive privilege of the dweller in the interior or among the hills, and compensates him for the absence of general society and those pastimes which the inhabitants of populous and wealthy towns provide for themselves. But those who have lived long in India seldom hesitate to give a preference to life in the Mofussil, for there is endless pleasure in shooting and hunting, and health is promoted by the activity they demand.

Jackall-hunting is a very good substitute for fox-hunting. At Calcutta it is pursued with much ardour. The jackalls are numerous, and in the cold mornings of November, December, January, and February afford a capital run. The hounds are chiefly imported from England, and are the produce of some of the best packs. The expense of importing them is considerable; but the Calcutta Hunt have never been chary of cost when thoroughly good dogs have been offered or despatched to them. The jackall is a great pest to the farmers and villagers; for like the fox in England, he commits great havoc among the poultry. His death, therefore, receives full sanction even at the expense of a few acres of wheat and rice-field trodden down in the chase.

The most popular sports in the interior are hog and tiger-hunting. Skill and courage are the indispensable attributes of the huntsman, and spears and rifles his necessary weapons; the spear for the boar, the rifle for the tiger. Englishmen altogether discard the German method of attacking the boar; they use neither fire-arms nor dogs. Mounted upon a nimble little Arab (in the west and south of India), or a gallant country-bred in the east and north-west, and having a long bamboo spear, they betake themselves to the skirts of a jungle or sugar-cane plantation and with beating heart and firm hand, await the rush of a sounder (a small herd or drove) of hogs, which have been turned out of their *franks*, by a posse of beaters armed with long sticks. It is not long before a fine boar makes his appearance. Scared at the sight of his enemies he rushes frantically across the open field. A hundred yards or less of law is given him, and away the hunts-men fly in hot pursuit. It is a race for the spear. He who comes up first with the hog and buries his spear-head in the grisly fellow's heart, wins the tusks, the coveted trophies of the chase. It is an even race so far, often over very rough and stony ground. The hog now begins to blow, he fears to fall from exhaus-tion without striking a blow; suddenly he slackens his pace, wheels round, and with a terrific snort charges his pursuers. This is the critical moment. One false thrust, one miss, and the boar's tusks rip up the horse or unseat the rider. But a single turn of the wrist will lift the sagacious Arab, in time, and as the boar rushes by, the spear is thrust into his shoulder; another thrust from the rival *chasseur* follows, and after an ineffectual struggle or two the gray patriarch of the sugar-cane *khet* (plantation), yields up his life-blood.

The story of one boar-hunt is the story of a thou-sand. It is only varied in the scene and in the number of the huntsmen, and the hogs. The chief localities of hog-hunting were the Deccan, and the centre of India. The progress of agriculture has tended to very materially reduce the range of the sportsman and to diminish the number of hogs, and now it is difficult to rear (or turn up) a sounder within many miles of the places where they once abounded. Still an occasional good run is to be had, and in lower Bengal a considerable number of pigs afford trophies to the Budge-Budge Hunt.

The flesh of the wild boar is much esteemed in India, but the sportsman prefers the possession of the tusks to any other fruits of his prowess in taking "first spear."

Tiger-hunting, the next in general favour, is pursued upon a different system to that adopted in the case of hog-hunting. It would not be safe to risk the encounter of a tiger on horseback. Elephants, therefore, are put into requisition, and are trebly useful in conveying the sportsman to the field, protecting him from the tiger's charge, and assisting in the destruction of the "feline monster."

A tiger's chief haunt is the jungle skirting a meadow or wheat land, where oxen either graze or draw the plough. It is seldom that a sortie from the jungle is not rewarded by the capture of a heifer or young buffalo. When, therefore, the death of a troublesome scourge of the herds is determined on, it is not unusual to bait the field with a cow, whose lowings at night attract the tiger. The latter sallies forth, seizes the prey, destroys it at once, and is found in the morning gorged to repletion by his nocturnal repast. The sportsmen, occupying howdahs on the backs of elephants, well armed with a couple of rifles each, which a servant keeps continually loaded, and provided with cigars, biscuits, and brandy-and-water, or pale ale, advance in line upon the tiger, and the moment he is sighted, salute him with a volley. Death, often, is the immediate result, and nothing then remains to be done but to provide the carcase with a carriage home, which is generally accomplished by throwing it over the back of an elephant, not already encumbered by a howdah. But very frequently the tiger is only wounded, or perhaps alarmed—then look out for a charge! With a growl and a roar, he springs upon the elephant, and has been known by his weight, to roll the latter, sportsman and all, on to the earth; a critical situation, from which the prostrate party are only rescued by a judiciously directed shot from a companion sportsman, who has just come up. If the elephant on the other hand can sustain his weight, the tiger makes an effort to reach the tenants of the howdah. This is a ticklish position, especially for the *mahout* or driver, who is seated on the elephant's neck, and has only the hankas or iron hook, with which he urges and directs the elephant's course, wherewith to defend himself. But if the danger of the sportsman is augmented by this charge, so also is the danger of the tiger. He has brought himself within a few feet of the deadly rifle, and it will be strange, indeed, if he escapes the shot directed at his *os frontis* or his chest. Instances have been been known of a tiger's tearing the sportsman from his seat, and bearing him away to the jungle, but these casualties are very rare. Ordinarily, the animal falls to the repeated shots, and is carried home that his skin, well dressed, may be converted into a rug or a howdah carpet, or despatched as a present to a loving friend at the Presidency or in England.

It is an unfortunate thing for a village when a tiger once carries off a peasant, for having tasted of human blood, his voracity becomes enormous, and he will not be easily contented with any other description of food.* Such tigers will establish themselves in some

* A tiger who destroys men is called, *par excellence*, a "man tiger." In the Saugor and Nerbudda territories the natives have an idea, that after a tiger has killed one man the rest of

narrow pass, where they lie in wait for passers by, men who carry the letter-bags, being their principal victims. Should there be any European stations at hand, the monster is soon sacrificed; but when the villagers can have no assistance of the kind, ten or twelve victims have been known to fall under the insatiable appetite of the savage, before the country has been sufficiently aroused against him, to take effectual measures for his destruction. A reward of five hundred rupees (fifty pounds), is sometimes offered by the native chief of a district, for the head of a tiger, that has become formidable to the people of a village; and a general muster of men and weapons, takes place in consequence of this stimulant to action. Having ascertained the haunt of the tiger, where he lies in wait, to spring from the bush, which forms his cover, on the unhappy passenger who endeavours to cross the path, the whole hunt assembles and the wilderness swarms with men; every tree is converted into a watch tower; the circle is formed, which, pressing in upon all sides contracts until, completely hemmed in, the tiger roused in his lair, and opposed in every direction, meets his death!

Like boar-hunting, tiger-shooting is rapidly declining as a sport, under the auspices of the ploughshare. In former times, there was no district in India more celebrated for its tiger-shooting than Goruckpore, near the Nepaul frontier. Year after year parties proceeded to its apparently inexhaustible Terai, and always returned with the spoils of numerous of these magnificent animals. In the time of Sir Roger Martin

mankind are safe, for the spirit of the man rides upon his head and conducts him to prey. They also believe that tigers without tails (for such there are—victims of accident, conflict, or disease) are men who have converted themselves into tigers by eating of a particular root, which effects the metamorphosis at once.

there was a well known tiger on the Nepaul frontier, who was the terror of the neighbouring villagers; man was his food, and he scorned to prey on any inferior animal. He once attempted to enter the hut of a Taroo, but the inmate received him with such a blow on the head from a Jungh axe, that the tiger was glad to retreat, and carried the scar of the wound to his dying day. By this scar he was known and recognised, and his depredations at last became so serious that Sir Roger Martin went out for the express purpose of killing him. He shot forty-eight tigers before he fell in with the one he was in search of, but the forty-ninth was "Le Balafre" himself, who fell, fighting to the last, and well supported his former character for ferocity.

Abbye Singh, the Rajah of Omorah, a very old and good sportsman, is known to have been at the death of nearly five hundred tigers; but it would be an endless task to enumerate all the instances in which large numbers of these animals have bit the dust, and yielded their skins as trophies to the sportsman. From the above, it can easily be imagined that tigers were "plentiful as blackberries" a few years ago; and it is easily accounted for. After the Nepaul war, the Terai was one wide inhospitable waste, without a vestige of inhabitants or cultivation, intersected by nullahs in every direction, and abounding in swamps; the jungles sprang up luxuriantly, and became the haunt of innumerable tigers, and wild animals of all descriptions. The annual inroads of sportsmen, and some slaughter by native shikarees did not apparently much diminish the number of the tigers; year after year they were killed in the same spots, and it appears that a desirable covert was no sooner vacated by the death of one, than another took possession of it, and a party was tolerably sure of good sport in the Goruckpore Terai.

It is very different now; the tigers would never have been extirpated by sportsmen; indeed, those killed bore such a small proportion to the whole number, that for some years no decrease appeared to have taken place. But it is the change in the Terai itself which has diminished them, and which bids fair very shortly to put a stop to tiger-shooting entirely. Where formerly there was a howling wilderness, now villages have sprung up, the land is cultivated, and the jungle cleared; the march of civilization has made inroads on the domains lately sacred to the tiger and the bear. English gentlemen have received grants of land from Government on clearing leases, and by their efforts the jungle is rapidly disappearing. Nor are the Nepaulese behind us; on their side of the boundary cultivation is increasing in a great degree, and the country daily becoming more densely populated. On the spot where a friend of the author's once killed a fine tiger, there is now a thriving village. The natural consequence of all this is, that the tigers have been obliged to retreat before the approach of civilization, and where formerly there were hundreds, you now will not find one; they have taken refuge in the lower range of hills, where they still find cover, but of course cannot be got at there. One may now pass through the Terai for miles without finding a good covert: the only shooting you are likely to see is a revenue surveyor "shooting the sun" with his theodolite; and instead of an account of the deeds of a tiger party, we get a report on settlements.

Elephant-hunting forms no part of an Englishman's sport on the continent of India. It is only in the forests of Coorg, in the peninsula, that the animals abound, and they are snared by the natives that they may be trained and domesticated. Sending two tame elephants into the jungle to decoy a wild one by their caresses, and driving them towards the spot where the ropes are disposed for his reception, the unfortunate beast finds himself in the coils, and in spite of all his fierce and powerful struggles, is bound fast, and kept on low diet until he can be carried away in triumph.

It is in the island of Ceylon that the elephant is the victim of the European rifle. Sallying forth with a good supply of ammunition, a sportsman will not have to proceed many miles into the interior before he comes upon herds of elephants grazing at their ease. He selects one for his prize, brings the deadly tube to bear upon a vital point, and the ponderous beast falls upon his knees and surrenders his life. If slightly wounded, he sees his enemy, and deeming he is to be reached, the elephant will come down at a thundering pace, trumpeting with his proboscis *en l'air.* A friendly tree will then afford cover for protection and another shot; still the animal advances, but when he is within a few yards of the object of his counter-attack, the latter slips aside and runs past the elephant. Too unwieldy to turn with ease and rapidity, the unfortunate animal again becomes a mark for the bullets of the rifleman, and after a few wild and ineffectual efforts to get at his persecutor, he dies, and his tusks are appropriated and sold.

Bear-hunting affords a good deal of sport, for Bruin is full of courage, and takes a great deal of killing. From the number of shot he will receive before he gives up the ghost, one would almost imagine that he bore a charmed life. The "sport" consists in the first instance, in finding the bear; in the second place, in evading observation and pursuit by him; and in the third, in shooting him under difficulties and risks. Bears are not often found in plains and level jungles: they affect mountains and rocky eminences, interspersed with ravines and dells. A friend of the author, who has had many opportunities of participating in the sport, gives the following description of the *modus operandi,* and the exciting scenes which attend upon the chase.

"The hunting of bears forms a favourite amusement with the few, who enjoy the violent exertion and excitement which it calls forth. As such sports are not common in India, few stations of the army affording the haunts of the bear in their immediate vicinity, it may perhaps be worth while to relate how it is carried on, especially as it is the most manly and interesting of field sports, and highly conducive to the health and active habits of those addicted to it.

"The sportsmen should be at least three in number, to pursue bears over rugged ground with any prospect of success. They must also be provided with about a dozen beaters, to roll down rocks into the glen, and start the game, and cannot take with them too many fire-arms, as, from the long distances at which it is necessary to fire, it is desirable to multiply the chances of killing; and the bear, besides, will seldom drop with a single ball, and when wounded is no despicable foe.

"The sportsmen having assembled at the ravine by break of day, two of them take possession of the hither brink of the ravine, while the third accompanies the beaters along the further verge, inciting them to shout and cast down masses of rocks into the gulf below. If Mr. Bruin happens to be outside his den he is generally aroused by this disturbance, and will be seen either at the very bottom, or making his way along the side of the precipice, by paths where the human head would whirl with giddiness and the human foot find no security. No time is to be lost in firing, as the bear having so decidedly the advantage in the race over ground for which nature and experience have particularly fitted him, the space between him and his pursuers increases at every moment. If not struck he will seldom turn, and there is little prospect of coming up with him, because the sportsman has every now and then to make a long detour to avoid broken ground, and is besides describing the outer curve, as it were, of a large circle, of which the bear occupies a position near the centre.

"If the bear be struck when near his pursuers, he will usually turn upon them, and then coolness is required not to throw away their fire until he approach so near as to give them the choice of the wound they shall inflict. On such occasions I would recommend the young sportsman to drop on his knee in taking aim, which by bringing him more nearly to a level with the bear, prevents the advance of that animal from materially altering the line of fire. If the beast be advancing directly upon him, and he be cool enough to allow him to approach within seven or eight paces, he cannot perhaps do better than aim at the space between its eyes, taking care not to throw his ball much higher than that, or it will pass harmlessly through the huge tuft of hair which overshadows the forehead, and crests its neck and shoulders. If the beast afford a side mark, let him, by all means, strike the point immediately behind the shoulder, bearing in mind that a great portion of the object presented to view, both above and below, consists of a shaggy fringe of long hair, susceptible of no damage from his weapons. A ball striking the ribs rarely fails more or less to disable the quarry, piercing either the heart, the lungs, or the liver. But even then he must be approached with caution, although he should appear dead or dying. The native servant of an officer was scalped and killed outright by a single blow from the paw of a wounded bear, which he approached under the idea that it was defunct. Owing to the deception the eye meets with in such ravines, the sportsman will miss his game much oftener than he thinks the distance warrants; and as he can never measure that distance afterwards, the mistake is not easily corrected, objects there appearing in general very much nearer than is really the case.

The ordinary charge of a gun at those long ranges would not carry a ball up with any certainty; and if the gun be of solid materials (and no other should be used in such break-neck places), two and a half drachms of powder will not be too much for a ball of eighteen to the pound.

"Double-barrelled guns at long ranges are not true to the aim taken along the plate, between the barrels; for each barrel being thicker at the breech than at the muzzle, slopes slightly inwards, so that the fire of the two will meet and cross at a certain distance. The difference, it is true, is not great; but when added to the various other considerations which affect the accuracy of ball practice at long ranges, it is of much importance."

The wild buffalo affords rare sport—in fact, there is none superior to it, from the ferocity and great strength of the animal, and the noble trophy his death places in the hands of his destroyer. The immense curved horns of the buffalo, sometimes measuring six feet in length, proudly decorate the hall of the sportsman who has been fortunate enough to slay one of the monsters. These buffalos are awfully destructive to the crops and the sugar-cane, and it is therefore under great circumstances of rejoicing that the ryot witnesses their immolation.

The chase of the deer in India admits of much variety. In Southern India greyhounds are employed in coursing antelopes. In Central India and the plains in the north-west, the *cheeta*, or hunting leopard, is used; while in the hills, where the deer are large and fierce, stalking is adopted, much upon the same principle and after the same manner with similar sport in the Highlands of Scotland. But many persons prefer shooting the deer, even in the plains, albeit, from the excessive vigilance and timidity of the race, it requires great caution and no inconsiderable degree of patience.

An extract from a letter from an old sporting friend to whom the author wrote a few years since for a hint or two upon the subject of deer-shooting, may not be unacceptable in this place.

"The best place for shooting deer, which I have been able to discover for the open plains, after some years' constant practice is, to circle them on horseback, taking care not to get too close, till you get the sun and wind in your favour. Having fixed on this desirable point, gradually close into it, the deer will be in a state of uncertainty; take your rifle from the bearer's shoulders, who is walking at your stirrup, and the moment the deer make up their minds to be off, dismount! Ay, ay! what a splendid buck—he turned round to see what you were doing; and as the sight of the rifle meets your eye, his clean, white breast is all before you, distant one hundred and fifty yards; one moment, and all the herd but him are scattered at their speed over the plain. Now pace the distance, and see if you judged correctly. Ay! one hundred and forty paces—not so bad! and the ball in the centre of the bottom of the neck. A deer standing, as I have mentioned, is, I think, the best mark; a rifle is generally held straight on the object, and a ball varies more in its elevation than it does sideways. An amusing way for two people is with double barrels. You spy a herd of deer a mile off; take your guns and canter away to the right and left, at a moderate angle from your people, who are to go straight on the herd; as you get towards the flank of the herd, gradually close in; they are getting alarmed, but looking at your men more than yourself. Judgment is now required when to ride fast or slow; now the leading doe makes a dash forwards, and all the rest follow her example; she stops, and so do they; you both gallop as they do, and stop when they do, and if the judgment is good, they will run between you, giving each sportsman two good shots."

A similar method of approaching the bustard is also recommended; he is a tall and timid bird; accustomed to the sight of the husbandmen with their plough, he does not seem disturbed by their approach. It is otherwise with the sportsman. The peculiarity of his costume arouses the apprehension of the bird, and he wings his flight beyond fowling-piece range the moment he sees his enemy. The best plan, therefore, is to employ a native ploughman or a hackery wallah with his vehicle to approach the bustard in concentric circles, diminishing the distance at each revolution. You accompany him, concealing yourself by the man's side, or behind his cart, and when within proper distance, level, and bring down your game.

# CHAPTER XII.

## RELIGIOUS CEREMONIES, CREEDS, &c.

*The Brahminical religion—The Doorga Poojah—The Nautch —Hindoo music — The Churuk Poojah — Juggernat'h — The Suttee—The Mohurrum—The Buckra Eade—The Bhearer.*

No better proof can be presented of the perfect and admirable toleration of the British rule in India, than the multitude of places of worship which may be seen at one view in any considerable town between Cape Cormorin and the Himalayas. The spire of the Christian church, in juxtaposition with the pagoda of the Hindoo, the dome, roof and lofty minarets of the Mahomedan mosque; the Parsee augiaree (or fire-temple), the Baptist Mission chapel, and the Greek church to which the Armenians resort, demonstrate that religious persecution is unknown, though political freedom may be under some restraint. It is by no means an uncommon thing to hear, early of a morning in any one of the cities, the bells of the Roman Catholic chapel and the Hindoo temple, forming with the cry of the muezzin from the summit of the minaret a not unpleasing concord. The bigots of all persuasions may detest each other, and manifest in their private intercourse the presence of strong religious prejudice, but no open demonstration of hostility is permitted. The law takes immediate cognizance of any violent ebullitions of hate; and this fear of the law holds even the passions of the fanatic in subjection.

The religion of the Hindoos, though based upon Brahminism, admits of many ramifications. Buddhism, an offshoot of Brahminism, possesses perhaps more votaries than any existing religion. Buddha, the ninth incarnation of Vishnu, "the illustrious lord of the universe," taught that the soul when sufficiently purified shall lose all consciousness of separate existence, and be received into the essence of the godhead. It teaches that this state of bliss is equally attainable by men, angels, and demons: it substitutes sanctity for sacrifice. The Jains, another branch of Brahminism, resemble the Buddhists in religious tenets, but look upon God as so inconceivable in his nature that the human understanding is too feeble to comprehend his perfections.

For purposes of religious and temporal government the early Brahmins instituted caste. Menu, the great Hindoo lawgiver, in all his writings insisted upon the importance of preserving the divisions of mankind intact; and to this time nothing is more terrible to a Hindoo than the risk of losing his caste by the wilful or accidental perpetration of some act which is inhibited to his sect. There are four original castes: The Brahmins, or priests; the Ksatriyes, or warriors. The Vaisyas, or merchants; and the Soodras, or vulgar to the first belongs, or belonged, the exclusive privileges of reading and explaining the sacred books, the Vedas. The warrior caste come next. Agriculture and trade, as third in order of importance according to the original constitution of society, constituted the pursuit of the Vaisyas; and the Soodras, to whom all knowledge of the Vedas was forbidden, filled all the menial and degrading offices. These four great castes have been infinitely subdivided, and as each minute subdivision acknowledges the protecting influence of some special deity or family of deities, the Hindoos have many thousands of slightly distinct forms of worship. It would be impossible to convey anything like an adequate idea of the mythology of the Hindoos within the compass of this volume, for the attributes of each special god and demi-god are infinite, and to our homely notions, gross and improbable. All the fabulous achievements ascribed by the heathen Greeks and Romans to the subjects of their Pantheon, rise into the possible by the side of the monstrous absurdities of the Hindoo creed. And their sculptured and modelled impersonations of their deities are as frightful and revolting as the major part of their belief. The ancients of Europe fitly associated their notions of super-excellence with the most beautiful embodiments. The perfection of the human form was deemed indispensable to the realization of the idea of supernatural power. The Jupiter, the Mars, the Apollo, and the Venus of the unknown sculptors who worked under the magic influence of religious enthusiasm, are examples of form and expression, which degraded and corrupt humanity never could completely attain. It is otherwise with the Hindoo. His sense of the powerful is of the vulgarest order. He gives an additional number of legs and arms to his destroyers and avengers, and connects their human attributes with portions of the limbs and heads of animals. He worships the energy of man and the fruitfulness of woman with unmistakeable symbols, and his idea of the godhead, Brahm, is only realized by three distinct heads, destitute of facial expression, each looking in a different direction.

In honour of these various tutelar deities, or patron saints, the Hindoo holds numerous festivals; on some of which occasions he makes great holiday. Indeed, so numerous are the holidays of the Hindoos, that at one time it was difficult to induce them to give their services to their employers for more than 200 days in the year. Certain imperative ceremonies of bathing and prayer are continually alleged as causes of unavoidable absence from business. At length the Government deemed it necessary to institute inquiries into the rigorous exactions of religion, and it was soon found that the threat of expulsion from office enabled the Hindoo materially to curb those devotional exercises, which amounted to mere form, if, in reality, they were practised at all. From fifty to one hundred festivals, the "red letter days" came down to twenty, and even these are now somewhat reduced. The great *poojas* (*pooja*, worship) are limited to two or three, and it is only upon the occasion of the *Doorga pooja*, or the *Dusserah*, as it is called in Western India, that some days of absence from all public duties are permitted.

A festival in honour of Doorga, or the goddess-consort of Siva, is the most splendid and expensive, as well as the most popular of any of the Hindoo festivals. It takes place in the month *Ashwinn* or *Assin* (the end of September or beginning of October).

The preliminary ceremonies occcupy several days, previous to the three days' worship.

During the whole of this period, all business throughout the country is suspended, and universal pleasure and festivity prevail. On the first of the three days of worship, the ceremony of giving eyes and life to the images takes place, before which they cannot become objects of worship. This is performed by the officiating Brahmin touching the cheeks, eyes, breast, and forehead of the image, saying, "Let the soul of Durga long continue in happiness in this image." Other ceremonies, and the sacrifice of numerous animals, as buffaloes, sheep, goats, &c., then follow. The flesh and blood of the animals, and other articles, are then offered to the images of the goddess and the other deities which are set up. The ceremonies and sacrifices of the second and third days of the worship are nearly similar to those of the first day. After the whole of the beasts have been slain, the multitude daub their bodies with the mud and clotted blood, and then dance like Bacchanalian furies on the spot. On the following morning, the image is, with certain ceremonies, dismissed by the officiating Brahmin.

This image—one of the most disgusting that can be conceived—represents *Kalee* (Doorga's impersonation of the Destroyer), a very black or blue female, having in one hand a scimitar, and in another the head of a giant, which she holds by the hair. Another hand is spread open, bestowing a blessing; and with the fourth she is forbidding fear. She wears two dead bodies for ear-rings, and a necklace of skulls, and her tongue hangs down to her chin—emblematic of her shame on discovering that, in her wild and ungovernable passion, she is trampling on her husband, Siva. The heads of several giants are hung in a girdle round her loins, and her tresses fall down to her heels. Having drank the blood of the giants she has slain in combat, her eyebrows are bloody, and the blood is falling in a stream down her breast; her eyes are red like those of a drunkard. She stands with one leg on the breast of her husband, and rests the other on his thigh.

This image is placed by the priests on a stage formed of bamboos, and carried, surrounded by a concourse of people of both sexes, and accompanied by drums, horns, and other Hindoo instruments, to the shore, and cast into the water in the presence of all ranks and descriptions of spectators; the priest, at the time, invoking the goddess, and supplicating from her, life, health, and affluence; urging her (their universal mother, as they term her) to go then to her abode, and return to them at a future time. During this period licentiousness and obscenity prevail. For three days of *worship* in Bengal the houses of the rich Hindoos are at night splendidly illuminated, and thrown open to all descriptions of visitors; and they acknowledge, with much attention and gratitude, the visits of respectable Europeans. The images exhibited on these occasions, are made of a composition of hay, sticks, clay, &c., and some of them are ten and twelve feet high.

During the whole of the day after the pooja, as some of the images are brought from villages at a considerable distance from the holy stream, in order to be cast in, the uproar and din are indescribable. Immense sums of money are expended on these festivals. A great deal is given in charity, and in feeding and clothing priests and beggars. Much is also spent in general feasting, and not a little is lavished on the *nautch girls*, or bayadéres, who dance before the goddess.

The NAUTCH is an Indian entertainment, of which dancing forms the chief element; not, however, where the guests dance, but where they witness certain evolutions dignified by the appellation of dancing.

The native of India does not condescend to Terpsichorean indulgence. He prefers to be a spectator of the gesticulations of others, who make a trade of the "light fantastic," and are called nautch girls.

These girls are of different kinds. The most respectable, according to the author of the "Vade Mecum," are the *meeraseens*, sometimes called *doominca;* though the real *doominca* exhibit in public before men, which the *meeraseens* never do. The word *meeras* means an *inheritance*, and *meeraseen* an *inheritress*, from the custom, in certain families, of never changing the set. As the *meeraseens* are never accompanied by male minstrels, they seldom play on other instruments than drums of different kinds, such as the *tabla*, *dholuk*, and *munjeera*; though the *meeraseens* never perform before assemblies of men, yet the husband and his sons may be present. They are modest and chaste in their manners and dress; but notwithstanding this, it sometimes happens that a fair *meeraseen* attracts the attention of the male part of the family. The *kunchenee* are of an opposite stamp: they dance and sing for the amusement of the male sex, and in every respect are at their command. They are attended by male minstrels, to whom they are often married. It is said these women always consider their first lover as their real husband during the rest of their lives; and, on his death, though they should be married to another, they leave off their pursuits for a prescribed period, and mourn agreeably to the custom of widows. They do not consider any part of their profession either disgraceful or criminal.

There are many other kinds of dancing women, such as, *hoorkenees*, *bazeegarnees*, *dharees*, &c. &c. In dancing, the nautch-girls present very picturesque figures, though somewhat encumbered by the voluminous folds of their drapery. Their attire consists of a pair of gay-coloured silk trousers, edged and embroidered with silver or gold lace, so long as only to afford occasional glimpses of the rich anklets, strung with small bells, which encircle the legs. Their toes are covered with rings, and a broad, flat, silver chain is passed across the foot. Over the trousers a petticoat of some rich stuff appears, containing at least twelve breadths, profusely trimmed, having broad silver or gold borders, finished with deep fringes of the same.

The *coortee*, or vest, is of the usual dimensions, but it is almost hidden by an immense veil, which crosses the bosom several times, hanging down in front and at the back in broad ends, either trimmed to match the petticoat, or composed of still more splendid materials, the rich tissues of Benares. The hands, arms, and neck, are covered with jewels, sometimes of great value, and the hair is braided with silver ribbons, and confined with bodkins of beautiful workmanship. The ears are pierced round the top, and furnished with a fringe-like series of rings, in addition to the ornament worn in England; the diameter of the nose-ring is as large as that of a crown-piece; it is of gold wire, and very thin; a pearl and two other precious gems are strung upon it, dangling over the mouth, and disfiguring the countenance. With the exception of this hideous article of decoration, the dress of the nautch-girls, when the wearers are young and handsome, and have not adopted the too-prevailing custom of blackening their teeth, is not only splendid but becoming; but it requires, however, a tall and graceful figure to support the cumbrous habiliments which are worn indiscriminately by all the performers. The nautch-girls of India are singers as well as dancers; they commence the vocal part of the entertainment in a high, shrill key, which they sustain as long as they can; they have no idea whatsoever of modulating their voices, and the instruments which form the accompaniment are little less barbarous; these consist of nondescript guitars, and very small kettle-drums, which chime in occasionally, making sad havoc with the original melodies, some of which are sweet and plaintive. The dancing is even more strange, and less interesting than the music; the performers rarely raise their feet from the ground, but shuffle, or to use a more poetical, though not so expressive a phrase, glide along the floor, raising their arms, and veiling or unveiling as they advance or describe a circle. The same evolutions are repeated, with the most unvarying monotony, and are continued until the appearance of a new set of dancers gives a hint to the preceding party to withdraw.

The passionate fondness of the natives for the nautch has in it something extraordinary. Many Europeans also were formerly so excessively devoted to it as to excite the special ridicule of a distinguished satirist. A few lines of his diatribe occur to us—

> "Shrilly she shrieked, and high above
> The music of her fiddles three,
> Rose the romantic strain of love,
> *Chota, chota, natchelee!*
>
> * * * *
>
> And then she danced! for so they call,
> Jingling her anklets while advancing,
> With many a horrid squeal and squall,
> With twirling hands and sudden kicks,
> Her charms of person much enhancing;
> People may patronise such tricks,
> But shouldn't, surely, call it dancing."

The music of the Hindoos consists of melodies; harmony is unknown. It (the music) is termed *surgeet.* The gamut is called *soorgum,* from the first four notes of the scale abbreviated. The number of tones is the same as in European music, with an infinite variety of semi-tones and quarter tones. The general term of melody is *rag* or *raggaree.*

The chief instrument of the nautch orchestra is the *vena.* It is strung with seven metal wires, three steel and four brass, but the melody is generally played on one of the steel wires. The other instrument is the *tom-tom,* or drum, an oblong hollow instrument of larger circumference in the middle than towards the ends. It resembles the small barrel used by fishmongers for the transport of presents of oysters.

There are twenty species of vocal compositions. The *dhoor pud* is the principal. It is the heroic song; the subject being generally the memorable actions of heroes; the style is masculine, easy, and free from ornament. The *holees* or *horees* are the common ditties which recite the amours of Krishna in the groves of Vrig. The *tuppa* is the favourite species of song; its subject is love. The tenor of the *tuppa* is one or more of the following themes: beseeching the lover to be propitious—lamentations for his absence—imprecations of rivals—complaints of inability to meet him from the watchfulness of the mother and sister-in-law—and the tinkling of the bells worn round the ancles, &c. In the tones of a Hindoo orchestra there is something peculiarly drowsy and discordant, but the natives prefer it infinitely to the European combination.

To proceed with the detail of native ceremonies—

The CHURUK POOJAH is a Hindoo festival deriving its name churuk (or *chakra*), a wheel or discus, from the circle performed in the swinging part of it, that terminates the annual ceremonies in honour of Siva. "The higher classes," says Williamson, "do not engage in it, although they contribute towards the expense of, and countenance it. The initiatory ceremonies of purification, abstinence, and exercises of devotion, take place several days before the commencement of the rites, during which time the *sunnyasees*, or worshippers, form themselves into parties, and wander about the streets with horns, drums, &c., making a most intolerable din. The first exhibition is that of suspension, which is performed by two posts being erected, on the top of which is placed a strong bar, from which the *sunnyasee*, or worshipper, is suspended by his feet over a fire kindled beneath him, into which rosin is occasionally cast. His head is then completely enveloped in the smoke, though sufficiently high to be beyond the reach of the flame. On the following day the *sunnyasees* dance and roll themselves upon the downy beds of various descriptions of prickly plants. Their next ceremony is called the *Jamp sanya*, or jumping on a couch of pointed steel, which has been thus described. A bamboo scaffolding of three or four stages is erected, on which the *sunnyasees* stand, tier above tier, the principal and most expert occupying the upper row, which is sometimes between twenty and thirty feet high. A kind of bedding, supported by ropes, is stretched beneath the scaffolding by a number of men. Upon the mattress are attached several bars of wood, to which are fixed very loosely, and in a position sloping forward, semicircular knives, upon which the *sunnyasees* throw themselves in succession. In general the effect of the fall is to turn the knives flat upon the bedding, in which case they do no harm, but occasionally severe wounds, and even death, are the consequences of this rite. Before they take their leap the performers cast fruits, as cocoa-nuts, bels, plantains, &c., among the crowd, among which there is a great scramble for them, as they are supposed to possess much virtue. Women desirous of progeny are very anxious to get these donations; and those of the first families send persons to obtain and bring them for their private eating.

The next is the day of the *churuk*, or swinging ceremony. Posts, about thirty feet in height, are erected in the suburbs of a town, across the upper part of which are loosely suspended long bamboos, so as to enable them to traverse freely. To one end of the bamboo two hooks are fixed by ropes, which are run through the fleshy parts of the back, near the shoulders. A rope is also fastened to the other end of the bamboo, which as soon as the party who is to swing is secured to the hooks, is pulled by several men, who thus raise the other end somewhat higher than the post. They then go round with it, with considerable velocity; by which means the man at the other end describes a circle of about thirty feet in diameter.

Sometimes a cloth is tied round the body, and secured to the hooks, to prevent, if the flesh should be torn away, the man from being dashed to pieces; but such is frequently not the case, and the party falling is often killed on the spot. Some of these men while swinging amuse themselves by smoking, and throwing fruit and flowers (which they take up on purpose), among the spectators.

On the morning following the *churuk*, Siva is worshipped in the temple, and the festival is concluded.

During each day of the festival, the *sunnyasees* worship the sun, pouring water, flowers, &c., &c., on a clay image of the alligator, and repeating *muntras*, or prayers.

Great efforts have been made by the missionaries and the British Government to put an end to these barbarous rites, and there can be little doubt that under the influence of education they will soon become mere matters of history.

But horrible as is the rite of churuk poojah it sinks into insignificance, or rises into humanity, by the side of the immolations which take place before the rolling car of Juggernat'h. Some account of this famous temple, its supposed origin, and the scenes which are enacted upon the occasion of the procession of Rath Jatra, may not be out of place here.

JUGGERNAT'H, in Hindoo mythology, is the reanimated form of Krishna. According to the Hindoos, the love-inspiring Krishna was one day shot with an arrow from the bow of a hunter, who left the lovely form of the deity, whom the Gopias had so franticly adored, to rot under the tree where it fell. After some time, his bones were collected by some pious persons, and made the means of enriching the priests of the Hindoos. Being placed in a box, they remained till Vishnu, on being applied to by a religious monarch, Indra Dhoomna, commanded him to make an image of Juggernat'h, and place the bones in it. The king would willingly have done as he was desired, but unfortunately, possessed not the skill for such an undertaking; so he made bold to ask Vishnu who *should* make it? Vishnu told him to apply to Viswakarma, the architect of the gods. He did so, and Viswakarma set about forming the image of Juggernat'h, but declared, if any person disturbed him in his labours, he would leave his work unfinished. All would have gone on well, had not the king shown a reprehensible impatience of those divine injunctions which he had solemnly pledged himself to observe.

After fifteen days he went to see what progress the holy architect had made, which so enraged him, that he desisted from his labours, and left the intended god without either arms or legs. In spite, however, of this perplexing event, the work of Viswakarma has become celebrated throughout Hindostan; and pilgrims, from the remotest corners of India, flock, at the time of the festivals of Juggernat'h, to pay their adoration at his monstrous and unhallowed shrine. Between two and three thousand persons are computed to lose their lives annually on their pilgrimage to Juggernat'h. The temples of this deity being the resort of all the sects of the Hindoos, it is calculated that not less than 200,000 worshippers visit the celebrated pagoda in Orissa, yearly, from which the Brahmins draw an immense revenue. All the land within twenty miles round the pagoda is considered holy; but the most sacred spot is an area of about 650 feet square, which contains fifty temples. The most conspicuous of these is a lofty tower, about 184 feet in height, and about 28 feet square inside, called the

Bur Dewali, in which the idol and his brother, and sister Subhadra, are lodged. Adjoining are two pyramidical buildings. In one, about forty feet square, the idol is worshipped; and in the other, the food prepared for the pilgrims is distributed. These buildings were erected in A.D. 1198. The walls are covered with statues, many of which are in highly indecent postures. The grand entrance is on the eastern side; and close to the outer wall stands an elegant stone column, thirty-five feet in height, the shaft of which is formed of a single block of basalt, presenting sixteen sides. The pedestal is richly ornamented. The column is surrounded by a finely-sculptured statue of Hanuman, the monkey-chief of the *Ramayana*. The establishment of priests and others belonging to the temple, has been stated to consist of 3,900 families, for whom the daily provision is enormous. The holy food is presented to the idol three times a day. This meal last about an hour, during which time the dancing girls belonging to the temple, exhibit their professional skill in an adjoining building. Twelve festivals are celebrated during the year, the principal of which is the Rath Jatra. Juggernat'h is styled the Lord of the World.

His temples, which are also numerous in Bengal, are of a pyramidical form. During the intervals of worship, they are shut up. The image of this god is made of a block of wood, and has a frightful visage, with a distended mouth. His arms, which, as he was formed without any, have been given to him by the priests, are of gold. He is gorgeously dressed, as also the other two idols which accompany him. In a compartment in the temple of Rama, he is represented in company with Bala Rama and Subhadra, without arms or legs.

The town of Juggernat'h is situated on the coast of the province of Orissa, in lat. 19° 49′ N., long. 85° 54′

E. It is named, and usually called Pooree, and is inhabited chiefly by the Brahmins, and others connected with the pagoda. On the sea shore, eighteen miles to the northward of Juggernat'h, are the remains of an ancient temple of the sun, called, in English, the black pagoda. The greater part of the temple is in ruins, having been thrown down, apparently by lightning, or earthquake,; but from what remains, it appears to have been one of the most singular edifices ever constructed in India. Part of the tower, 120 feet high, is still standing, and the antechamber, or *jungmohun*, about 100 feet high.

This temple, which has been long deserted, was built by a rajah of Orissa in 1241.

"Historians have often remarked the surprising resemblance which exists in the external worship of India and Egypt. In the religions of both countries, bloody and unbloody sacrifices; the strict observance of pilgrimage, causing a numerous assembly of people at festivals, penances, bathing in supposed holy waters, and if drowned, the act supposed to confer eternal bliss; their gods conveyed from one temple to another on enormous stages, erected upon huge cars. These latter customs, related by Herodotus (forming part of of a long comparison between the Hindoos and Egyptians, admirably set forth in Heeren's "Researches)," are particularly applicable to Juggernat'h.

At Pooree, about the middle of every year, three large cars are built for the Rath Jatra, at which festival the images take "an airing" as far as Gondicha Hour, or god's country-house, a mile and a half distant: "the cars are dragged by Kattabethias, or coolies, and by thousands of other people." But apparently, it must be the peculiar duty and privilege of these people to draw the cars.

The images are placed in their respective positions by the Dytas, or charioteers of Juggernat'h. "The car of Juggernat'h is forty-five feet in height; it has sixteen wheels of seven feet diameter, and a platform thirty-five feet square. The *ruth* of Bulbhudra is forty-four feet high; it has fourteen wheels of six and a half feet diameter, and a platform thirty-four feet square. The car of Subhudra is forty-two feet high; it has twelve wheels of six feet diameter, and a platform thirty-three feet square. A small rail, about eight inches in height, nearly surrounds the platform of each *ruth*. An opening is left of a few feet in front of the idol."

"The entire scene of the Ruth Játra savours, to an incredible extent, of the ludicrous, the barbarous, and the awful. The eager expectation, the unceasing din of a great multitude, the acclamations of "Victory to Juggernat'h!" which rend the ear, when the images are brought forth, in an erect posture, or rather *rolled* forth, by means of iron handles fastened in their backs, and exposed to the stupid gaze of the delighted people.

"There you may picture to yourself Christianity shuddering; there, morality weeping. Momus is not to be found there—the God of Mirth has slunk away trembling; as for intellect, she slumbers in silence, awaiting the dawn of a better day.

"The ponderous machines are set in motion; they creak while the creatures strain the cables in the midst of their joy and madness. There they are—

'All around, behind, before,
With frantic shout, and deafening roar;
And the double double peals of the drum are there,
And the startling burst of the trumpets blare;
And the gong, that seems, with its thunders dread,
To astound the living, and waken the dead.'

"But all their enthusiasm has soon subsided; and on the termination of the festival, many of that once delighted multitude either retire to die, or reach their deserted homes the victims of ignorance, poverty, and wretchedness.

"It is, perhaps, useless to state here that human sacrifices under the wheels of the car have long been abolished."*

The suppression of the rites of the car of Juggernat'h is not the only service rendered to humanity by the British Government.

SUTTEE, female immolation on the funeral pile of a deceased husband, once very common—was put down in 1828 by Lord W. Bentinck. Although the *Shastras* recommend, and contain regulations for the practice of the rite, the sacred ordinances not only do not expressly, as some had supposed, enjoin it, but distinctly point out in what manner a woman, after the decease of her husband, shall be taken care of; and leave it optional with her, either to burn herself, or live a future life of chastity and respectability. If, they say, after marriage her (the woman's) husband shall die, her *husband's* relations—or, in default thereof, her *father's*—or, if there be none of either, the magistrate, shall take care of her; and, in every stage of life, if the person who has been allotted to take care of a woman, and do not take care of her, each in his respective stage, the magistrate shall fine them.

The ordinance nevertheless adds, that *it is proper* for a woman to burn herself with the corpse of her husband; in which case she will live with him in Paradise three crore and fifty lacs, or thirty-five millions of years. If she cannot burn, she must observe an inviolable chastity. If she remain always chaste, she will go to Paradise; if not, she will go to Hell. Immediate beatitude, an almost immortal life in hea-

* See a very elaborate and interesting account of Orissa and the temple of Juggernat'h, from the pen of Lieut. Laurie, of the Madras Engineers.

vens of ineffable delight, and other enjoyments, whose gross sensualities are concealed by the dazzling brilliancy of oriental colouring, are among the irresistible charms which are held forth to enthral the mind, and lead the victim of marital selfishness too often to become a *suttee.* In short, it is averred, that the gods themselves reverence and obey the mandates of a woman who becomes one. There is, besides these, another powerful motive which operates in conjunction with them. Among the Hindoos a woman, after the decease of her husband, loses entirely her consequence in his family, and is degraded to a situation little above that of a menial. She is told that if she become a *suttee,* she will not only escape from that life of assured debasement and contempt, but will ascend to a state as pre-eminently exalted; and will thus (whatever the crimes of the parties may have been) save both her own soul, and the souls of her husband and her husband's family, from purgatory and future transmigration.

These doctrines, impressed on the minds of weak women by a designing priesthood, were in the olden time sufficiently convincing to lead to much personal immolation. Drugged and excited, the victim went to her death with an air of heroism, and the deafening noise of *tom toms,* the crackling of the faggots, and the shouts of the multitude, drowned her cries and shrieks until the destructive power of the flames reached her heart. The harvests of the Brahmins on these occasions were considerable. Fees were paid and feasts given by the woman's friends, and as she ascended the pile she distributed her trinkets among the priests.

Without pretending to rigid accuracy of computation, I should say that about one-fourth of the entire population of India are of the Mahomedan persuasion. Vast numbers of the sepoys, public and private servants, sailors, shopkeepers, western agriculturists, pedlars, the horsemen in the service of native chieftains and in the irregular cavalry of our own service, are Mahomedans. Especially in the centre and north-west of Hindostan, the mosque occurs as frequently as the Hindoo pagoda, and a lively hatred is cherished by the followers of the prophet towards the idolatrous disciples of Brahma. It is not, however, so strongly manifested in their intercourse with each other as to lead to any breaches of the peace. There is, perhaps, more real animosity between the sects of Mahomedanism, for each looks upon the other as an apostate, or the representative of a principle calculated to shake the consistency of the creed, and this hostility is most powerfully manifested in some of the public ceremonies and processions,—the most remarkable of which is the *Mohurrum*.

The annual celebration of the *Mohurrum* in all large Mahomedan communities of the Sheah sect, though, strictly speaking, a fast of the most mournful kind, is accompanied by so much pomp and splendour, that strangers are at some loss to distinguish it from festivals of pure rejoicing. The Sheahs, who are settled in Hindostan, are in some degree obnoxious to the charge of introducing rites and ceremonies, almost bordering upon idolatry, in their devotion to the memory of the Imaums Hossein and Houssein.

Imbibing a love of show, from long domestication with a people passionately attached to pageantry and spectacle, they have departed from the plainness and simplicity of the worship of their ancestors, and in the decorations of the *tazees* (mimic tombs), and the processions which accompany them to the place of sepulture, display their reverential regard for Ali and his sons in a manner which would be esteemed scandalous, if thus accompanied, in Persia and Arabia, where the grief of the Sheah is more quietly and soberly manifested.

Several processions take place during the celebration of the Mohurrum. At Lucknow, on the fifth day, the banners are carried to a celebrated shrine or *durgah* in the neighbourhood to be consecrated, it being supposed that the standard of Hossein, miraculously pointed out to a devout believer, is preserved at this place. The veneration in which this sacred relic is held, nearly equalling that which in some places in Europe is displayed towards pieces of the true cross, affords another proof of the corruption of the Mahomedan religion by the Sheah sect of India. The *durgah* at Lucknow is not only visited at the commemoration of Hossein's obsequies, but prayers and oblations are offered in its holy precincts upon recovery from illness, or any other occasion which calls for praise and thanksgiving.

The gifts deposited at the *durgah*, consisting of money, clothes, and other valuable articles, become the property of the officiating priest, who is expected to disburse the greater portion in charity. All the Moslem inhabitants of Lucknow are anxious to consecrate the banners employed at the Mohurrum, by having them touched by the sacred relic; and for this purpose, they are conveyed to the shrine with as much pomp and ceremony as the circumstances of the proprietors will admit. A rich man sends his banners upon elephants, surrounded by an armed guard, and accompanied by bands of music. The arms and accoutrements, representing those worn by Hossein, are carried in some of these processions; and one of the most important features is Dhull Dhull, the horse slain with his master on the fatal field of Kurbelah: his trappings are dyed with blood, and arrows are seen sticking in his sides. Multitudes of people form these processions, which frequently stop while the moollahs recite the oft-told, but never-tiring story, or the tragic scene is enacted by young men expert at broadsword exercises; and as Hossein is surrounded and beaten down, muskets are fired off, and shouts and beatings of the breast attest the sincerity with which his followers bewail his untimely end. On the seventh night of the Mohurrum, the marriage of Hossein's daughter with her cousin, a faithful partizan of the house of Ali, is celebrated with much pomp and show. The procession of the marriage of the unfortunate Cossim and his ill-fated bride is distinguished by trays bearing the wedding presents, and covered palankeens, supposed to convey the lady and her attendants; the animals employed in the cavalcade, with the exception of the favoured Dhull Dhull, are left outside the walls; but the trays containing sweetmeats, &c., a model of the tomb of Cossim, and the palankeen of the bride, are brought into the interior, and committed to the care of the keepers of the sanctuary until the last day, when they make a part of the final procession to the place of interment.

The most extraordinary feature, however, in the commemoration of the deaths of Hossein and Houssein, is the participation of the Hindoos, who are frequently seen to vie with the disciples of Ali in their demonstrations of grief for the slaughter of his two martyred sons, and in the splendour of the pageant displayed at the anniversary of their fate. A very large proportion of Hindoos go into mourning during the ten days of the Mohurrum, clothing themselves in green garments, and assuming the guise of fakeers.

The complaisance of the Hindoos is returned with interest at the Hooly, the Indian Saturnalia, in which the disciples of the prophet mingle with the heartiest good will, apparently too much delighted with the general license and frolic revelries of that strange carnival, to be withheld from joining it by horror of its heathen origin. The ceremonials observed at the celebration of the Mohurrum are not confined to processions out of doors; persons of wealth and respectability having an Imaum-barrah constructed in the interior of their own dwellings. This is usually a square building, containing a hall and other apartments, in which the mourning assemblages during the period of the festival are congregated. It is decorated for the time with all the splendour which the owners can afford. The *tazee* is placed upon the side facing Mecca, under a canopy of velvet or tissue richly embroidered; and near it there is a pulpit, very handsomely constructed of silver, ivory, ebony, or carved wood, having a flight of stairs covered with an expensive carpeting of broad cloth, velvet, or cloth of gold.

The *tazee* is lighted up by numerous wax candles; and near it are placed offerings of fruit and flowers, presented by pious ladies to do honour to the memory of the Imaums.

The remainder of the hall is fitted up with considerable splendour, furnished with mirrors, which reflect the light from numerous lustres, lamps, and girandoles. Poorer persons are content with less glittering ornaments; and in all, an assemblage is held twice a day, that in the evening being the most imposing and attractive. The guests are seated round the apartment; the centre of which is occupied by a group of hired mourners, consisting of six or eight persons.

These men are usually of large stature, and of considerable muscular strength. They are very scantily clothed in a drapery of green cloth, their breasts and heads being perfectly uncovered. A moollah, or priest, selected on account of his superior elocution, ascends the pulpit, and proceeds to the recital of a portion of a poem in the Persian language, which contains a detailed account of the persecution and tragic fate of the Imaums. The composition is said to be very pure; and its effect upon the auditory is prodigious.

After some well wrought passage, describing the

sufferings of the unhappy princes, the reader pauses, and immediately the mourners on the ground commence violently beating their breasts, and shouting "Hossein! Hossein!" until at length they sink exhausted on the ground amid the piercing cries and lamentations of the spectators. A part of each day's service consists of a chant in the Hindostanee language, in which the whole assembly join; and the Sheahs end it by standing up and cursing the usurping Caliphs by name, devoting the memory of each offending individual to universal execration. The Soonnees hold these solemn assemblies; but their grief at the cruel sufferings of so many estimable members of the prophet's family does not assume so theatrical a character. Attired in the deepest mourning, they evince the most profound sorrow; and it is persons of this persuasion who manifest the greatest indignation when there is any risk of their processions being crossed by the heathen revelries of the Hindoos.

The pomps and ceremonies which precede it are nothing to the grandeur reserved for the display on the last day of the Mohurrum, when the *tazees* are borne to the place of interment. This pageant represents the military cavalcade of the battle of Kurbelah, together with the funeral procession of the young princes, and the wedding retinue of the bride and bridegroom divorced by death upon their nuptial day. The banners are carried in advance, the poles being usually surmounted by a crest, composed of an extended hand, which is emblematic of the five holy personages of the prophet's family, and a symbol particularly designating the Sheah sect. Many make a declaration of their religious principles by holding up the hand; the Soonnee displays three fingers only, while the Sheah extends the whole five. The horse of Prince Hossein and his camp equipage appear furnished with all the attributes of sovereignty; some of the *tazees*, of which there is a great variety, are accompanied by a platform, on which three effigies are placed,—the ass Borak, the animal selected by Mahomed to bear him on his ride to heaven, and two houries. The tomb of Cossim, the husband of Hossein's daughter, is honoured by being carried under a canopy; the bridal trays, palankeens, and other paraphernalia, accompany it, and the whole is profusely garlanded with flowers.

These processions, followed by thousands of people, take the field at break of day; but there are so many pauses for the reading of the poem dedicated to this portion of the history of the events of Kurbelah, and such numerous rehearsals of Hossein's dying scene, that it is night before the commencement of the interment. Devout Mussulmans walk, on these occasions, with their heads and their feet bare, beating their breasts, and tearing their hair, and throwing ashes over their persons with all the vehemence of the most frantic grief; but many content themselves with a less inconvenient display of sorrow, leaving to hired mourners the task of inciting and inflaming the multitude by their lamentations and bewailments.

The zeal and turbulence of the affliction of Ali's followers are particularly offensive to the Soonnees, who, professing to look upon Hossein and Houssein as holy and unfortunate members of the prophet's family, and to regret the circumstances which led to their untimely end, are shocked by the almost idolatrous frenzy displayed by their less orthodox brethren; and the expression of this feeling often leads to serious disturbances, which break out on the burial of the *tazees*. Private quarrels between the sects are frequently reserved for adjustment to this period, when, under pretext of religious zeal, each party may make an assault upon his enemy without exposing the real ground of his enmity. In a few places which border the Ganges or Jumna, the *tazees* are thrown into the river; but generally there is a large piece of ground set apart for the purpose of the burial. It is rather a curious spectacle to see the tombs themselves consigned to earth, with the same ceremonies which would attend the inhumation of the bodies of deceased persons; the *tazees* are stripped of their ornaments, and when little is left except the bamboo frames, they are deposited in pits. This ceremony usually takes place by torchlight, the red glare of innumerable flambeaux adding considerably to the wild and picturesque effect of the scene.

The followers of Mahomed have another annual festival called the *Buckra Eade,* or goat sacrifice. Claiming to be descendants of Abraham, through his son Ishmael, whom they aver to have been chosen for the offering to the Almighty, and not Isaac, they celebrate the event. It is commemorated by the sacrifice of particular animals: camels, sheep, goats, kids, or lambs, according to each person's means; this is supposed to answer a double purpose, not only honouring the memory of Abraham and Ishmael, but the sacrifices assisting in a time of great need.

It is supposed that the entrance to Paradise is guarded by a bridge made of a scythe, or some instrument equally sharp, and affording as unstable a footing. The followers of the Prophet are required to skate or swim over this passage, and it will be attended with more or less difficulty, according to the degree of favour they have obtained in the sight of Heaven.

The truly pious will be wafted over in safety, but the undeserving must struggle many times, and be often cut down in the attempt, before they can attain the opposite side. In this extremity, it is imagined that the same number and kind of animals, which being clean, and esteemed fitting for sacrifice, they have offered up at the celebration of the *Buckra*

*Eade,* will be in waiting to convey them in safety along the perilous passage of the bridge.

Under this belief, the richer classes of Mahomedans supply their poorer brethren with goats and sheep for the sacrifice ; a work of charity, incited by the purest motives, and which, if not possessing all the efficacy ascribed to it, at least furnishes the poor man's home with an ample and a welcome feast; for though poverty compels the lower classes of Mussulmans to imitate the Hindoos in the frugality of a vegetable meal, they never refuse meat when it is procurable.

The BHEARER is another annual Mahomedan *fête.* It takes place at night. It is instituted in honour of the escape of an ancient sovereign of Bengal from drowning; who, as the tradition relates, being upset in a boat at night, would have perished, his attendants being unable to distinguish the spot where he struggled in the water, had it not been for a sudden illumination caused by a troop of beauteous maidens, who had simultaneously launched into the water a great number of little boats, formed of cocoa-nuts, garlanded with flowers, and gleaming with a lamp, whose flickering flame each viewed with anxious hopes of a happy augury. The followers of the king, aided by this seasonable diffusion of light, perceived their master just as he was nearly sinking, exhausted by vain efforts to reach the shore, and guiding a boat to his assistance, arrived in time to snatch him from a watery grave. This is the common, though not the universal interpretation of the origin of the festival.

Whatever may have been the motive of its institution, the scene which is exhibited on the occasion of its celebration is exceedingly beautiful. The banks of the Ganges are brilliantly lighted up on the evening of the festival, and numerous flights of rockets announce the approach of a floating palace, built upon a raft, and

Fortress of Alli Ghur.

preceded by thousands of small lamps, which cover the surface of the water, each wreathed with a chaplet of flowers. The raft is of considerable extent, formed of plantain trees fastened together, and bearing a structure, which Titania herself might delight to inhabit. Towers, gates, and pagodas, appear in fantastic array, bright with a thousand colours, and shining in the light of numberless glittering cressets.

# CHAPTER XIII.

## ARCHITECTURE, TEMPLES, MONUMENTAL REMAINS, &c.

*The cave-temples—The river-temples—The character of Hindoo sculpture—Futtehpore Sikri—Deeg—Secundra—Tomb of Hoomaioon—Agra—The Taj Mahal—Lucknow, &c.*

WERE the grandeur of the native governments of India to be judged by the architectural remains which still decorate different parts of the country, a lofty impression would be entertained of the early civilization of the Hindoo and Mahomedan rulers. From the southernmost points of the Peninsula to the vicinity of Delhi, majestic temples, gorgeous palaces, and splendid tombs, are still extant, in various stages of decay, each attesting a vastness of design and a delicacy of execution which scarcely find a parallel in the stupendous works still seen on the banks of the Nile, and in the vicinity of the Tigris and Euphrates. Ancient Egypt and Mesopotamia may have exceeded other countries in the dimensions of the abodes and the sepulchres of their kings, but they are fairly rivalled in India by the exquisite taste of the architects who flourished under the Mahomedan dynasties, or who embodied the conceptions of the founders of the Brahminical system of worship.

In Southern India, because more remote from the seats of Mahomedan government, Delhi, Lahore, Oude, &c., the Hindoo temples are the main objects of attraction. Some of them are of great height, covering two or three acres of land, and divided into an infinite number of apartments.

But perhaps the most extraordinary specimens of Hindoo architecture are the cave-temples in Western India and the Deccan. Ellora, Ajunta, and Elephanta, are the most remarkable, and were probably constructed because their freedom from external climatic influences, and their concealed positions, which reduced the chances of their being despoiled by the bigots of other creeds, ensured to them a greater permanence.

The cave-temples of Ellora—or Verrool, as the place is called by the natives—are situated about a mile from the ancient Mahomedan city of Dowlatabad. In magnitude and execution they excel every thing of the kind in India. They comprise several temples, and are filled with figures, some dedicated to Siva, and some to Boodh. As far as can be ascertained, these temples were constructed 2,500 years since, but the Brahmins assign to them a much more extravagant antiquity, going even 2,000 or 3,000 years higher than the date assigned by us, according to the Scriptures, to the creation of the world.

The temples of Ajunta are by no means so extensive as those of Ellora, but they are exceedingly curious, and afford an excellent idea of the taste and talent of the Hindoo sculptors of the olden time.

The other cave-temples are near the island of Bombay, on Salsette and Elephanta.

The little island of Elephanta, the true name of which is Shapooree, derives the Portuguese appellation from a huge stone elephant, about three times as large as life, which stands in a field about a quarter of a mile to the right of the usual landing-place. The elephant is rudely sculptured, and is so much dilapidated by climate as to leave little beyond a rough outline of the animal it is intended to represent. From the landing-place a steep and narrow path leads up the hill, winding prettily through woods and on the banks of precipices for about three-quarters of a mile, when, after passing a ruined portico, supported by two pillars and two pilasters, we reach the entrance to the great cavern, magnificently situated for the prospect which it commands. The cave is excavated out of the solid rock, the roof being supported by pillars which once exhibited traces of beautiful carving and architectural taste. The form of the interior of the cave, which was evidently a temple dedicated to Siva, is that of a cross, and not unlike the plan of a basilica.

At the upper end is an enormous bust, with three faces, looking in different directions, and reaching from the pavement to the ceiling. It was at one time supposed to represent the Trimurti, or Hindoo Trinity—Brahma, Vishnu, and Siva; but more recent discoveries have ascertained that Siva himself, to whose worship and adventures most of the other ornaments of the cave refer, is sometimes represented with three faces, so that the temple was evidently consecrated to him.

In the interior of the continent, and more especially in Upper and Central India, the pagodas and sculptured rocks are very numerous, and illustrative of the extensive character of the mythology of the Hindoos. At the confluence of rivers, on the summit of lofty hills, at the base of prodigious rocks in secluded places, the traveller constantly comes upon singular remains, attesting at once the vigorous conceptions and religious zeal of the statuaries. Near Oojein, in the province of Malwa, for instance, are some splendid vestiges of sculpture. At Oomerkantuck, in the province of Gondwana, at the source of the rivers Soane and Nerbudda, there is a temple said to have been built by one of the ancient rajahs of Butturpore, and to contain an image of Bhavani, under whose name the consort of Siva is worshipped in that part of the country. In Guzerat also are ruined temples, originally of great magnitude; and from the source to the mouths of the Ganges are not less than 3,500 edifices of various dimensions consecrated to Gunga, the goddess of the river, and some of these date back two or three centuries, when the fervid zeal of the Hindoo defied the relentless persecution of the Mahomedan. Gunga is the personification of the sacred stream. The honour of giving birth to that goddess has been claimed for their deities both by the Shivas and Vishnaivas, the former alleging that she sprang from the locks of Siva—the latter that she issued from the foot of Vishnu. According to either, she came to restore to King Suguin the 60,000 sons whom the deity Brigu had caused his wife to have at one birth, and who, for some malpractices, had been reduced to ashes. In her passage towards the sea she was swallowed by a holy sage for disturbing him in his worship; but by some channel or other she contrived to make her escape, and having divided herself into a hundred streams (now forming the Delta of the Ganges), reached the ocean, when, it is fabled, she descended into Palata to deliver the sons of Suguin. All castes of the Hindoos worship this goddess of their sacred stream. Clay images are set up in the temples to her honour. The waters of the river are highly reverenced, and are carried in compressed vessels to the remotest parts of the country, from whence also persons perform journeys of several months' duration to bathe in the river itself. By its waters the Hindoos swear in our courts of justice. A person, by either bathing in or seeing the river, may be as much benefited as if he had visited all the places of worship on its banks. For miles near any part of the banks of the sacred stream, thousands of Hindoos of all ages and descriptions pour down every night and morning to bathe in or look at it. Persons in their dying moments are carried to its banks to breathe their last, by which means the deaths of many are often accelerated; and instances have been known wherein such events have thereby been actually produced. Several festivals are held during the year in honour of Gunga; and then the bathing, especially at the junction of the main stream with a tributary, is universal.

To return to the temples, some of singular form and character are erected on the rises of the Kistna river, near Mahabuleshwur, a range of hills in Western India; and their situation is not less worthy of remark than their structure and *materiel.* Although knowing little of painting, and not much more of poetry, if we except their ancient lyric songs of Sanscrit origin, the Hindoos have yet an eye so true to nature (when not called upon to imitate it) that their temples are ever found commanding the most lovely and attractive views. At Mahabuleshwur, a fine arch, cut in one of the basaltic temples, permits the rich foliage of the mountains to be seen at its back, as well as the exquisite landscape that forms the foreground of the picture.

Of the temple of Juggernauth we have elsewhere spoken—in the chapter on religious ceremonies, &c.—and for a minute scientific account of the character of Hindoo architecture, its stages, and most remarkable extant illustrations, the reader is referred to the elaborate and interesting work of the late Major Kitto, of the Bengal army, and the Journal of the Asiatic Society. The following unpublished observations upon Hindoo sculpture generally are deserving of attention for their truth and originality. They are from the pen of a travelled officer of the Bengal Engineers of great taste and experience—

"The new city of Bujrungghur becomes visible after a passage of some ten miles of extremely wild and rugged road (on the way from Agra to Mhow in Malwa), and just at the point from which it appears, is a statue of Mata Devi, in high relief upon a stone placed upright on the left-hand side of the road. It has few of the horrible accompaniments peculiar to that fearful goddess, and is designed to represent a beautiful woman in an attitude calculated to display the figure. Though a little overstrained, it is the most spirited attempt I have seen of the Hindoo's chisel on this rough rock, and excepting the figures of Gopris (or nymphs), the most graceful.

"In the features of the face, Hindoos always fail, therefore nothing is ever to be expected in that department; but in the more ancient of their sculptures, the figures are sometimes ably executed.

"And here I cannot forbear remarking, that the Hindoos bear an undue imputation of indecency in their religious sculpture. There can be no doubt that temples do exist wherein the most abominable representations abound; the reports of travellers have testified to this, and it is very possible, that in the peninsular countries, the taste may be more depraved than in Upper Hindostan. But I can affirm that in marching from Cawnpore to Agra, Meerut, Kurnaul, Simla, and thence through Delhi and Jypore, to Mhow in Malwa, and the banks of the Nerbudda, and from thence again through Oojyne hither, a distance of about 1,400 miles, I have not met with even one obscene image, although I have lost no opportunity of inspecting works of art, of whatever nature, on the road; I of course except the Phallus or Lingam, the symbol of Mahadeo as god of nature, which is to be found in every village and under every considerable tree in Malwa. And I consider that there are good grounds for this exception, and that to regard it as a proof of the pruriency of the Hindoo imagination is both unwise and uncharitable; although doubtless its origin may be attributed to the most depraved taste in the originator. In the first place, it is so unlike that of which it is a symbol, that unless informed of its meaning, it would be impossible to conjecture it, nineteen out of twenty of these symbols being mere shapeless masses of rock placed upright under a bingut or peepul tree, and those which are chiselled being almost as unmeaning. And secondly, the habit of regarding it from infancy as a religious emblem must tend to prevent any connection with it of impure ideas. Add to this, that the notions and habits of natives of this country, whatever their rank, birth, or real modesty, are so utterly unsoftened by delicacy, according to our notion of that word, that not an expression, however literally coarse, in the compass of a language eloquent in a certain species of anatomy, is considered as too large, or too rude for the most gentle lips. And a woman, who would sacrifice herself to a most fearful death to escape a breach of chastity, would, in the innocence of her heart, utter expressions which would assure her the unrivalled sway of Billingsgate. This familiarity with all the arcana of European polish, however revolting, however objectionable upon other accounts, does certainly tend to rob of its dangerous tendency any symbol such as that under discussion. Nor can I doubt, while I reprobate the system of Lycurgus, which sought to destroy by familiarity the pruriency of the imagination, that it was so far a successful, though a most ungraceful expedient, and one that, by uprooting personal bashfulness, and with it all our dreams of female sacredness and reverence, and in rendering common what is chiefly desired as rare, had a fatal tendency to divert the passions from their natural course, and beget an indifference in particulars wherein the most exclusive nicety should prevail."

The architectural remains of the Mahomedans are not, of course, of the same antiquity as those of the Hindoos, and can hardly be said to have any connection with religion. They consist chiefly of palaces, tombs, serais, and halls of justice. The greater portion are in Upper India. A few may be described:—Futtehpore Secree, lying about twenty-four miles from Agra, is celebrated for the mausoleum of Sheikh Saleem. The town, such as it is, stands upon the back of a narrow ridge of sandstone hills, rising abruptly from the alluvial plains, to the highest about 150 feet; and extends three miles north-north-east and south-south-west. The origin of the celebrity of the place is thus described by Colonel Sleeman. The Emperor Akbar's sons had all died in infancy, and he made a pilgrimage to the shrine of the celebrated Moin-od-deen, of Cheest, at Ajmere. He and his family went all the way on foot, at the rate of three coss, or four miles a day, a distance of about three hundred and fifty miles. Kunauts, or cloth walls, were raised on each side of the road, carpets spread over it, and high towers of burnt brick erected at every stage, to mark the places where he rested. On reaching the shrine, he made a supplication to the saint, who at night appeared to him *in his sleep*, and recommended him to go and entreat the intercession of a very holy old man, named Sheikh Saleem, who lived a secluded life upon the top of the little range of hills at Secree. He went, accordingly, and was assured by the old man, then ninety-six years of age, that the Empress Jodh Baee, the daughter of a Hindoo prince, would be delivered of a son, who would live to a good old age. She was then pregnant, and remained in the vicinity of the old man's hermitage till her confinement, which took place 31st August 1569. The infant was called after the hermit, Mirza Saleem, and became in time Emperor of Hindostan, under the name of Jehangeer. It was to this Emperor Jehangeer, that Sir Thomas Roe, the ambassador, was sent from the English court. Akbar, in order to secure to himself, his family, and his people, the advantage of the continued intercessions of so holy a man, took up his residence at Secree, and covered the hill with magnificent buildings for himself, his courtiers, and his public establishments. The quadrangle, which contains a mosque on the west side, and the tomb of the old hermit in the centre, is perhaps one of the finest in the world. It is 575 feet square, and surrounded by a high wall, with a magnificent cloister all around within. On the outside is a magnificent gateway, at the top of a noble flight of steps, twenty-four feet high. The whole gateway is one hundred and twenty feet in height, and the same in breadth, and presents beyond the wall five sides of an octagon, of which the front face is eighty feet wide. The arch in the centre of this space is sixty feet high by forty wide. The gateway is extremely grand and beautiful, composed of red sandstone, with inlaid decorations of marble; but the beholder is struck with the disproportion between the thing wanted and the thing provided. There seems to be something quite preposterous in forming so enormous an entrance for a poor diminutive man to walk through; and walk he must unless he is carried through on men's shoulders; for neither elephant, horse, nor bullock, could ascend the flight of steps. "In all these places the staircases, on the contrary, are as disproportionately small. They look as if they were made for rats to crawl through, while the gateways seem as if they were made for ships to sail under." The tomb of Sheikh Saleem, the hermit, is a very beautiful little building, in the centre of the quadrangle. It once boasted a great deal of mosaic ornament, but the Jâts, when they reigned, removed it all.

At Deeg is a noble quadrangular garden, constructed by the Jâts during their ascendancy. It is 475 feet long by 350 feet wide; and in the centre is an octagonal pond, with openings on four sides leading up to four buildings, which stand in the centre of each face of the garden. These buildings are justly accounted the most beautiful Hindoo edifices for accommodation ever erected. They are formed of a very fine ground sandstone, brought from the quarries of Roopbas, which are eight or ten miles south-west of Futtehpore Sikree. These stones are brought in in flags, some sixteen feet long, from two to three feet wide, and one thick, all sides as flat as glass, the flags being of the natural thickness of the strata. The openings spoken of above have, from the centre of the pond to the foot of the flight of steps leading from them, an *avenue* of *jets d'eau.*

At Secundra, a few miles from Agra, is the magnificent tomb of Acbar. It stands in a square area of about forty English acres enclosed by an embattled wall, with octagonal towers at the angles, surmounted by open pavilions, and four very noble gateways of red granite, the principal of which is inlaid with marble, and has four high marble minarets. The space within is planted with trees and divided into green alleys, leading to the central building, which is a sort of solid pyramid, surrounded externally with cloisters, galleries, and domes, diminishing gradually on ascending it, till it ends in a square platform of white marble, surrounded by most elaborate lattice work of the same material, in the circle of which is a small altar tomb, also of white marble, carved with a delicacy and beauty which do full justice to the material and to the graceful forms of Arabic characters which form its chief ornament. At the bottom of the building, in a small but very lofty vault, is the real tomb of this great monarch, plain and unadorned, but also of white marble.

Delhi contains in its immediate neighbourhood some beautiful mosques and other edifices in good preservation. There is the Jumma Musjeed, the mausoleum of Hoomaioon, and the Kootub Minar. The latter is a lofty pillar or minaret, deriving its appellation from Kootuboodeen (the pole star of religion), who under the Emperor Mahomed Ghori became a mighty general, and ultimately achieved the throne, and was the first of the Patan or Affghan sovereigns. The circumference of the pillar measures 143 feet, and its height was formerly between 200 and 300 feet, but the upper part being struck by lightning and destroyed, it now only reaches about 110 feet.

The tomb of Hoomaioon, about six miles from Delhi, through masses of ruins, is a noble building of granite inlaid with marble, and in a very chaste and simple style of Gothic architecture. It is surrounded by a large garden, with terraces and fountains, all now gone to decay. The garden itself is surrounded by an embattled wall with towers or minarets, four gateways and a cloister within, all the way round. In the centre of the square is a platform of about twenty feet high and about two hundred feet square, supported also by cloisters, and ascended by four flights of granite steps. Above rises the tomb, also a square, with a great dome of white marble in its centre. The apartments within are a circular room, in the centre of which lies, under a small raised slab, the unfortunate prince to whose memory the fine building is raised. In the angles are smaller apartments where other branches of his family are interred.

The Jumma Musjeed, or principal mosque of Delhi, is a superb building in excellent repair. It is elevated very advantageously on a small rocky eminence to at least the height of the surrounding houses. In front it has a large square court, surrounded by a cloister open on both sides, and commanding a view of the whole city, which is entered by three gates, with a fine flight of steps to each. In the centre is a great marble reservoir of water, with some small fountains, supplied by machinery from the canal. The whole court is paved with granite inlaid with marble. On its west side, and rising up another flight of steps, is the mosque itself, which is entered by three noble Gothic arches surmounted by three domes of white marble. It has at each end a very tall minaret. The size, the solidity, and the rich materials of this building, place it nearly at the head of all the specimens of Mahomedan architecture now extant.

But unquestionably the most beautiful monument in Hindostan is the Taj Mehal, erected near the city of Agra. It is a magnificent tomb, constructed at the instance of the Mogul Emperor, Shah Jehan, in commemoration of his beautiful queen, Noor Jehan, the Light of the World. The building was designed by Austin de Bordeux, a Frenchman of great talent and merit, in whom the emperor placed great reliance. It cost 3,174,802*l.*, and occupied 20,000 labourers and architects for twenty-two years. The building stands upon the north side of a large quadrangle, looking down into the clear blue stream of the river Jumna, while the other three sides are enclosed with a high wall of red sandstone. The entrance to this quadrangle is through a magnificent gateway in the south side, opposite the tomb; and on the other two sides are very beautiful mosques, facing inwards, and corresponding exactly with each other in size, design, and execution. That on the left, or west side is the only one that can be used as a place of worship, because the faces of the congregation, and those of all Mahomedans, at their prayers, must be turned to the tomb of their prophet—to the west. The mosque on the east side was therefore, built merely as a companion to the other. The whole area is laid out in square parterres, planted with flowers and shrubs in the centre, chiefly the cypress, all round the borders, forming an avenue to every road. These roads, or paths, are all paved with slabs of freestone, and have, running along the centre, a basin, with a row of *jets d'eau* in the middle, from one extremity to the other. The quadrangle is from east to west 964 feet, and from north to south 329. The mausoleum itself, the terrace upon which it stands, and the minarets, are all formed of the finest white marble, inlaid with precious stones. The wall around the quadrangle, including the river face of the terrace, is made of red sandstone, with cupolas and pillars of the same white marble. The inside of the mosques and apartments in and upon the walls are all lined with marble or with stone-work that looks like marble; but on the outside the red sandstone resembles uncovered bricks. The dazzling white marble of the mausoleum was brought from the Jeypore territories, a distance of 300 miles, upon wheeled carriages. What was figuratively said of Augustus may be literally said of Shah Jehan: he found cities all brick, and left them all marble. The emperor and his queen lie buried side by side in a vault beneath the building, to which access is obtained by a flight of steps. Their remains are covered by two slabs of marble, and directly over these slabs, upon the floor above, in the great centre room under the dome, stand two other slabs, or cenotaphs, of the same marble, exquisitely worked in mosaic. Upon that of the queen, amid wreaths of flowers, are worked in black letters, passages from the Koran. Upon the slab over the emperor there are none: merely a mosaic wall of flowers and the date of his death.

The cause of the difference is, that Shah Jehan had

himself designed the slab over his wife, and saw no harm in inscribing the *words of God* upon it; whereas, the slab over himself was designed by his more pious son, Aurungzebe, who did not think it right to place there "holy words" upon a stone which the foot of man might some day touch.

Noor Jehan, the Light of the World, or, as the inscription on her tomb calls her, Ranoo Begum, the ornament of the palace, died in 1631; her husband in 1666. She died in giving birth to a daughter, and on her death-bed made two requests; first, that Shah Jehan would not marry again after her death, and get children to contend with hers for his favour and dominions; and secondly, that he would build for her the tomb with which he had promised to perpetuate her name.

Both her dying requests were granted. Her tomb was commenced upon immediately. No woman ever pretended to supply her place in the palace, nor had Shah Jehan children by any other.

The city of Lucknow, the capital of the kingdom of Oude, contains a great many noble specimens of architecture, the most striking of which are the tombs of Nabob Saadut Ali, the gate of Roum (Constantinople), and the Imambarra, or cathedral. This last grand mosque consists of two courts rising with a steep ascent, one above the other. It contains besides the mosque a college for instruction in Mussulman law, apartments for the religious establishment maintained there, and a noble gallery, in the midst of which, under a brilliant tabernacle of silver, cut glass, and precious stones, lie buried the remains of its founder Asuph ad Dowlah. The whole is in a very noble style of eastern Gothic, and is remarkable for richness and variety, as well as for the proportions and general good taste of its principal features.

At the city of Benares, the holy city of the Hindoos,

and at Ajmere in central India, are some beautiful specimens of architecture, especially at the latter, where there is a tomb to the memory of a celebrated Mahomedan saint, one Sheik Kajah Mooadeen. Thousands of Mussulmans make pilgrimages to this tomb to implore the blessing of male offspring. It is of white marble inlaid with gold and silver. A similar tomb is found at Currah, between Allahabad and Cawnpore. It was erected to the memory of one Camaul Sheikh. The architecture is grave and solemn, consisting of a square tower pierced on each front with elegantly formed and carved Gothic doorways, and surmounted with a dome of a very judicious form, and harmonizing with the general character of the building, not being semicircular, but conical, and in the form of a Gothic arch. Besides this large chapel are many raised tombs, to the memory of the sons and disciples of Camaul Sheik, who appears to have been a person of great sanctity.

Briefly, India abounds with monumental remains, and when all that England has accomplished, in the architectural way, shall have crumbled to the dust, the majestic works raised three or four or more centuries ago, by Hindoos and Mussulmans, will survive to attest the sublimity of their conceptions, and the munificence of their expenditure.

# CHAPTER XIV.

## THE CHIEF TOWNS OF INDIA.

*Calcutta, Madras, and Bombay—Delhi—The Great Mogul—Agra—Lucknow—Benares—Hyderabad.*

PRESUMING that the reader of these pages is destined for one or other of the three great presidencies, it is not impossible that a slight sketch of the characteristics of each of the great towns will be acceptable.

CALCUTTA, as the metropolis of British India, is by far the largest and most populous of the towns. It stands upon the left bank of the river Hooghly. The approaches to it, between the rich and and well-wooded banks of a winding river, are extremely picturesque, entirely shading the town from view, until the vessel which is bound for Calcutta is within a quarter of a mile from its anchorage. Here the whole splendour of the town at once bursts upon the view. The Government House with its vast dome and ornamental gates, the churches with their lofty spires, the public offices and enormous private dwellings, all faced with white stucco, relieved by green Venetians, the handsome ghauts, or landing places, the suspension bridge over a rivulet which encircles the town, the ramparts of Fort William bristling with guns, the tall column erected to the memory of Sir David Ochterlony—all serve to impress the spectator with exalted notions of the magnificence of the City of Palaces—an impression which a closer inspection and greater familiarity serves to dissipate. Before, however, Calcutta is seen, we pass between the magnificent gardens of spacious suburban villas, not unlike some of the handsome residences which fringe the Thames, in the vicinity of Richmond and Thames Ditton. These are, for the most part, on the left bank of the river, but on its opposite stands the Botanical Garden of the East India Company, adorned with many of the finest tropical productions—trees of stupendous altitude, and a banian tree, whose shadowing branches extend over two or three acres of ground. Here also is Bishop's College, an elegant Gothic structure of a quadrangular form, like most of the buildings of the same character in Oxford and Cambridge, but not joined at the angles, the southern side of the square being also open to the river, thus exhibiting the buildings of the northern side as the most conspicuous objects from the opposite bank. The north side of the building is composed of a central tower, which is in height sixty-five feet—in depth, from north to south, twenty-five feet. The right, or western, side of this tower is occupied by a building of equal depth, but whose height is but forty feet, and its length, from east to west, sixty feet—the ground floor of which is the hall. The upper floor is the library of the college. The left, or eastern, side of the central tower, is occupied by the chapel, a building of the same dimensions with the preceding, but in every other respect altogether dissimilar: being, of course, a single compartment, with an arched roof, in its exterior figure and decorations approaching to a miniature resemblance of that superb structure, King's College Chapel, in

Palace of Sujah Dowlah, at Lucknow.

Cambridge. The ground floor of the central tower forms an entrance both to the chapel and the hall. The first floor is the vestibule of the library. The two wings, extending from north to south, to the length of 150 feet (equal to that of the northern side described above), are allotted to the residence of professors, pupils, and domiciliaries. The edifice cost above 13,000*l.*

The college is founded for a principal and two other professors from the English Universities, and as many students as can be maintained, either on the proper foundation of the incorporated society, or on the endowment of any other religious society of the Established Church, or of the local governments, or individuals. The students are educated either as missionaries for the extension of Christianity in its present form, and in the mode of ancient discipline and order which is alone recognised by the Church of England, or as schoolmasters for the dissemination of general and useful knowledge.

Landing at Calcutta, we find that between the fort and the town, immediately opposite the anchorage, is an extensive plain, called a *Maidaun*, along one side of which runs an aqueduct, and on three sides of it a handsome broad road, which of an evening is crowded with vehicles of all descriptions, and innumerable equestrians. We now have an opportunity of inspecting the principal buildings. These consist of the Town Hall, a spacious edifice wherein public meetings are held, balls and public dinners given; the Sudder Dewanee Adawlut, or principal Court of Justice, the Supreme Court, the Bengal Club, the principal market, the Racket Court, the offices of the Adjutant and Quarter-Master-General, and several private dwellings. At the southern extremity of the eastern range of buildings stands the jail, and contiguous to it a large hospital, and the race-stand—for where the Maidaun terminates the race-course begins. Near to this spot also rises St. Paul's Cathedral.

This beautiful structure, a monument of the Christian piety and zeal of the Right Rev. Dr. Wilson, Bishop of Calcutta, was eight years in course of erection.

The first stone was laid on the 8th October, 1839. The funds were obtained by the Bishop, either by subscription, or from his own private purse; the entire expense being about 50,000*l.*

Her Majesty the Queen, at an audience granted to the Bishop when last in England, was pleased to approve highly of the ground plan and elevation of the cathedral, and to present a superb set of silver gilt plate for the service of the Holy Communion. Her Majesty had previously condescended to sanction the gift of the painting of the Crucifixion, by West and Forrest (originally designed for St. George's Chapel, Windsor, in 1787, by his late Majesty King George the Third), to St. Paul's Cathedral. The centre part of this picture now adorns the great eastern window of the choir.

His Grace the Archbishop of Canterbury convened a meeting at the Palace, Lambeth, in March, 1840, for opening a subscription in aid of the design, which his Grace honoured with his own subscription of 200*l.*

The Hon. East India Company made a grant of 15,000*l.* in February, 1840, besides the gift of the site, and the appointment of two Chaplains.

The University of Oxford presented books for the Cathedral library to the value of 200*l.*, and also 300*l.* in money.

The Venerable Incorporated Society for Propagating the Gospel in Foreign Parts, made a grant of nearly half a lakh of rupees for founding a Native Canonry.

The Society for Promoting Christian Knowledge presented 5,000*l.* and a superb folio Bible and Prayer-book.

The British and Foreign Bible Society gave twelve beautifully bound large quarto Bibles.

A relative of the late Rev. John Natt, of St. John's College, Oxford, and Vicar of St. Sepulchre's, London, contributed 4,000*l.* to the Endowment Fund, and 750*l.* for a Canon's residence.

A lady of North Wales presented 1,000*l.*

The Rev. Mr. Craig, of Leamington, presented a Lectern, in the form of a brazen eagle, with expanded wings, after the model of those in the cathedrals at home.

Mr. Llewellyn, late of Calcutta, presented an alabaster model of the Cathedral, executed in Italy, five feet in length by two feet in height, which the Bishop has given to the University of Oxford, and which is deposited on a suitable base in the Picture Gallery of the Bodleian Library.

Captain Kittoe provided a most handsome stone font, eight and a half feet each way at the base.

The cathedral of Calcutta will gradually become a native or mission church, for service in the vernacular languages. The mission has begun wisely and cautiously; and is intended to be of a peculiarly learned and staid character, as connected immediately with the bishop and clergy of the cathedral.

There is no doubt that it will be a kind of guardian to the other missions in our Church in the diocese, tending to animate what is good in them, and to check anything approaching to what is unsuitable or injudicious.

The style of the architecture is the English perpendicular Gothic, with a few variations, occasioned by the climate; it is, in fact, Indo, or Christian Gothic. The tower and spire are built after the model of the admired Norwich Cathedral, with improvements suggested by that of Canterbury. Most of the details of the ornaments, externally and internally, are taken from the finest specimens of York Minster.

The building is constructed of a peculiar kind of brick, specially prepared for the purpose. It is dressed with Chunar stone, and well covered and ornamented inside and out with *chunam*, which takes a polish like marble.

The sacred edifice was consecrated on Friday, October 8, 1847, being the anniversary of the day when the first stone was deposited in 1839.

The whole edifice is not larger than many of the fine old parish churches in England, as Saffron Walden, Halifax, Southwell, Manchester; but it is as large as the necessity of the case requires. And a district or parish church having been urgently wanted for twenty-five years, it has been merely distributed in all its parts so as to meet the special purposes of a cathedral, and it is furnished and fitted up with that end in view.

Turning back and proceeding into the interior of the town, in a northerly and easterly direction, we find many stately buildings, all announcing either the commercial importance of Calcutta, or the ample means of the inhabitants, the liberal spirit which has contributed to the foundation of public institutions, or the tolerance which prevails in religious matters. There is the Metcalfe Hall, a splendid edifice, raised in memory of Lord Metcalfe, who, as acting Governor-General, crowned a long and brilliant career of usefulness and honour, by giving freedom to the press of India. In this hall, is an extensive public library, the museum and library of the Asiatic Society, and the offices and rooms of the Agricultural Society. Then there are Writers' Buildings, a long range of chambers, in front of which is a spacious tank called the Loll Diggie, fringed with trees, the Custom House, the Mint, a building of classical form and of great extent, boasting a machinery corresponding with that of the Royal Mint on Tower-hill, London; the Bank of Bengal; the extensive premises of the auctioneers; Protestant and Roman Catholic churches, Mahomedan mosques and Hindoo pagodas; a Jesuit's College, once a handsome theatre; the Medical College, one of the finest architectural ornaments of the city; the Hindoo and Madrissa (or Mahomedan) college; and a number of chapels, offices, and masonic lodges. In the interior also we find large and commodious hotels, numerous shops, as large as the largest in Regent-street, especially the coachmakers, booksellers, upholsterers, jewellers, and general shopkeepers. All these, intermingled with private dwellings, impart a grandeur to the town, which loses nothing of its importance in the activity of a thriving population of 250,000 persons.

Calcutta is abundantly supplied with good water and excellent markets. It is under the management of a municipal committee, and boasts an active police. The health of the town is much looked after, and if it were lighted with gas, no city in Europe would stand a comparison with the proud City of Palaces.

As the whole country around Calcutta is perfectly level, there is little of beauty in the suburbs excepting upon the river's banks. At a distance of twelve miles stand the handsome barracks of the Artillery, at Dum Dum. Sixteen miles off, through a delicious park where the Governor-General has a residence, lies the Barrackpore cantonment, where there are generally five or six regiments quartered. To these places, and to certain factories and villas within a circuit of twenty miles, the denizens of Calcutta occasionally resort for recreation and change of air, but the temptation to leave the town, in other respects, is very slight.

MADRAS, the capital of the Presidency of that name, is the town next in importance to Calcutta. It stands upon the Coromandel coast, and is the emporium of the trade from Cape Comorin upwards. Fort St. George, which stands immediately upon the shore contiguous to the town, protects the roadstead and the town.

Landing at Madras is a service of danger. A tremendous surf rolls towards the shore, with so much force at certain seasons of the year, that if the greatest care were not taken by boatmen, their craft must inevitably be swamped. The passage between ships and the shore is effected in large barges called *Massoollah boats*, rowed by three or four pairs of oars. They have awnings for the purpose of enclosing passengers, who sit deep in the boat. As the boat approaches the land the boatmen watch the roll of the waves, and pulling as near to the shore as possible, leap out of the craft and drag it high and dry before the next breaker can assail it. There is a class of vessel called the *catamaran*, which consists merely of a log or two of wood, across which the boatman, if he may so be called, sits paddling himself to and fro. If he is capsized, an event which never can happen to his primitive vessel, he immediately scrambles on to the catamaran again, and resumes his work. These men, wearing conical caps, are very useful in conveying notes and parcels to passengers, when communication by larger boats is impossible.

The houses at Madras, standing upon the sea-shore, are of white and pale yellow stucco, with verandas and Venetian blinds. The absence of all shade is very striking, and to the eye at first offensive. The rest of the houses of the town, belonging to the gentry, stand in large compounds, scattered over a considerable extent of ground, and mingled with gardens. Some of the roads, especially the Mount Road leading to St. Thomas's Mount, are broad and well kept, but cannot escape being exceedingly dusty in the dry season of the year. The Government House is handsome and has a banqueting-house attached, and here very large parties are given upon occasion. The Madras Club is,

General View of Madras.

however, the most striking edifice. It is a very extensive building designed for the accommodation of a great number of persons, under admirable regulations, and at a moderate expense. It has entirely superseded the necessity for hotels: such as are to be found here are small and miserably furnished and attended. A statue to Sir Thomas Munro, formerly Governor of Madras, and two statues in honour of the Marquis Cornwallis, attract the attention of visitors; and those who are destined to remain at Madras, soon become interested in the great number of useful and charitable institutions with which the town abounds. Among these are the Madras College, the Medical College (which contains 120 pupils), the Orphan Asylum, the Mission, Charity and Free Schools, the Philanthropic and Temperance Associations, the Masonic Lodges, the Moneygar Choultry (a species of *serai*), the private seminaries, the institutions for the education of native females, &c. The churches are numerous at Madras, several excellent newspapers are published, and there are large establishments or shops where everything that humanity, in its most civilized state, can require is to be had for the money. Messrs. Pharaoh, Franck, and Ashton, will supply you with a paper of pins, a chandelier, or a steam-engine—a library of books, a pot of anchovies, and a carriage and pair. The prices at which the productions of Europe are sold, are by no means high, considering the expense of carriage to India, warehousing, insurance, establishment, the interest of money, &c. Very large fortunes are made in trade in Madras, and it is remarkable that, while Calcutta has experienced a great many vicissitudes, some of which have scattered ruin and desolation throughout society, the Madras houses of business, by a steadier system, have remained unscathed.

Bombay comes third in order of importance, but it is a town of greater interest and activity than Madras, and has the advantage of a most picturesque and beautiful situation. The harbour well deserves the appellation which the Portuguese bestowed upon it of *bomo-baio*, or "good bay." The island projects from the Malabar coast, with which it is connected by a tongue of land, or causeway—now converted into a railroad. The lofty western ghauts rise, as it were, immediately above it, and form one side of the bay. The town is enclosed within a fortress, constructed after Vauban's first system, and between it and the native town is an extensive esplanade, suited to military operations. A good many Europeans reside in the town—the houses of which are lofty, spacious, and handsome; but the major part of the opulent inhabitants occupy mansions beyond the native town, as the picturesque localities of Mazagon (so famous for its mangoes), Bycullah (where there is a club, a church, and a race-stand), Girgaum, Malabar Hill, Breach Candy, &c. The Governor resides, when he is in town, at Parell, a magnificent and commodious house, three or four miles from the fort, standing on a slight elevation. Connected with Bombay by a causeway, is the small island of Colabah, where there is a church, many pretty villas, and barracks for a European regiment. A light-house and observatory terminate the island.

Some of the buildings of Bombay are fine, and their purposes excellent. There is the Elphinstone College, founded in honour of Mountstuart Elphinstone, once governor of the island and dependencies—a college where hundreds of natives have been admirably educated; a medical college, established by the late Sir Robert Grant; St. Thomas's Church, the Mint, and the Town Hall. The latter is a superb and classical edifice, where the sittings of the Supreme Court are held, and balls, concerts, &c., given. It is likewise the place of public assembly, and the meetings of the committees of the different societies. The Bombay branch of the Asiatic Society has an immense and well-chosen library and a museum; but books may also be obtained at the "Europe shops," where everything else is vended. The bazaars are not very handsome, but well supplied; there is a theatre, where amateurs occasionally act; enormous cotton screws, a spacious hotel, commercial houses and offices upon a grand scale, and an infinite variety of places of worship. The Roman Catholic chapels and churches are more numerous here than in any other part of India, as the descendants of the early Portuguese visitors abound. Mosques and Hindoo temples are constantly found contiguous to each other, and here the Parsees—the descendants of the Guebres, or fire-worshippers, who fled from Mahomedan persecution to India—have their *augiaree*, or fire temple, where the sacred fire is constantly kept up by the priests, who receive, from pious Parsees, through the grating which encloses the silver stove, offerings in the form of sandal wood. There are few statues in Bombay, but the churches contain handsome monuments, and there are some busts and pictures in the Town Hall and the rooms of the Societies and Institutions.

There is probably no place in the world which contains such a motley population as the town and island of Bombay. Strolling, towards the evening, either on the esplanade, or in the vicinity of the Town Hall, you may encounter Banians (pedlars and merchants), Persian and Arab horse-dealers, Parsees, descendants of the Guebres, Chinese, Portuguese, Armenians, Hindoo clerks, coolies, Abyssinians, Europeans, infantry, cavalry and artillery soldiers, &c. All live in perfect harmony, for all enjoy the benefit of the greatest toleration in the exercise of their several religions.

Nor is the diversity of objects confined to the people who perambulate the town. There is much variety in the vehicles in use. While the natives who are in good circumstances, move about in all sorts of queer carts and cars, the Europeans patronize buggies—a covered kind of gig—landaulettes, chariots, britzkas, and *shrigampoos*. The last named is a square carriage, something like a palankeen on wheels, and being surrounded by Venetian blinds, is a cool and agreeable means of locomotion.

Of the towns in the interior the most remarkable are Delhi, Agra, Lucknow, Benares, Hyderabad, and Ajmere. Dinapore, Cawnpore, Poona, Meerut, Bangalore, Bellary, Belgaum, and similar places, owe their importance to the cantonments which form a considerable part of the towns themselves, and which are maintained by the towns. They consist, for the most part, of bungalows in compounds, bazaars, and places of worship; those which are on the banks of the Ganges having likewise warehouses and handsome ghauts. Patna and Mirzapore, on the Ganges, are also towns of some extent, where a considerable trade is carried on with the lower provinces of Bengal. At Patna are large opium godowns, for here the poppy is grown, and the opium extracted, forming a large article of export to China. The opium is the exclusive property of the Government, by whom it is sold to the merchants and brokers at public auctions. It has been the source of immense fortunes to many persons, and a fountain of trouble to the Government; for the attempt to force it upon the Chinese, resulted in an expensive war.

DELHI, the ancient capital of the Emperors of Hindostan, is still the residence of their lineal descendants. The "Great Mogul," however, with whose "effigies" all card-players are more or less familiar, has long been entirely bereft of all political authority. He is now a mere pensioner; but the officers of Government offer him all the external marks of courtesy pertaining to the regal office; and when European or native you to recommend him very kindly unto him. Our cape-merchants name is M. William Edwards, an honest gentleman, that useth me with verie loving respect.

Dear M. L. W., conveigh these twoe letters that I have sent to you, to the parties to whom they are directed: my poore mother and mine unckle Williams. You may do me a kinde office to desire him (with such convenient termes and patheticall perswasions as your discretion shall dictate and suggest unto you) to remember me as his poore industrious peregrinating kinseman, neerest unto him in blood of all the people in the world; to remember me, I say, with some competent gratuitie, if God should call him out of the world before my returne into my native countrie. I praie you, if hee be living, and doth use to come to London as he was wont to doo, that you would deliver my letter to him with your owne hands, and not send it unto him.

You may remember to relate this unto your friends that I will now mention as a matter verie memorable: I spent in my ten moneths travels betwixt Aleppo and the Moguls court but three pounds sterling, yet fared reasonable well everie daie; victuals beeing so cheape in some countries where I travelled, that I oftentimes lived competentlie for a pennie sterling a day. Yet of that three pound I was cousened of no lesse then ten shillings sterling by certaine lewd Christians of the Armenian nation; so that indeed I spent but fiftie shillings in my ten moneths travailes. I have beene in a citie in this countrie, called Detee [Delhi], where Alexander the Great joyned battell with Porus, K[ing] of India, and conquered him; and in token of his victorie erected a brasse pillar, which remaineth there to this day.[1]

Pray remember my humblest service to the Right

[1] Terry, in his 1655 edition (p. 81), says: 'I was told by Tom Coryat (who took special notice of this place) that he, being in the city of Dellee, observed a very great pillar of marble, with a Greek inscription upon it which Time hath almost quite worn out, erected (as he supposed) there and then by great Alexander, to preserve the memory of that famous victory' [over King Porus]. Roe also mentions this monument (*Embassy*, p. 103), no doubt on Coryat's authority. The reference seems to be to the Asoka pillar described by Finch (*supra*, p. 156). It is of stone, not of brass as stated in the text.

from this, the midland parts therof being watered by divers channels of the famous Ganges, which I have not as yet seene, but (God willing) I meane to visite it before my departure out of this countrie, the neerest part of it beeing not above twelve daies journy from this court. The King presenteth himselfe thrice every daie without faile to his nobles ; at the rising of the sunne, which he adoreth by the elevation of his hands ; at noone ; and at five of the clocke in the evening. But he standeth in a roome aloft, alone by him selfe, and looketh uppon them from a window that hath an embroidered sumptuous coverture, supported with two silver pillasters to yeeld shaddowe unto him. Twice every week elephants fight before him, the bravest spectacle in the worlde. Many of them are thirteene foot and a halfe high ; and they seeme to justle together like two little mountaines, and were they not parted in the middest of their fighting by certaine fire-workes, they would exceedingly gore and cruentate one another by their murdering teeth. Of elephants the King keepeth 30,000 in his whole kingdome at an unmeasurable charge ; in feeding of whom, and his lyons and other beasts, he spendeth an incredible masse of money, at the least ten thousand pounds sterling a day.[1] I have rid upon an elephant since I came to this court, determining one day (by Gods leave) to have my picture expressed in my next booke sitting upon an elephant.[2] The king keepeth a thousand women for his own body, whereof the chiefest (which is his Queene) is called Normal.

I thinke I shall here after this send another letter unto you before my departure out of this countrey, by a worthy man, which is the minister and preacher of our nation in this place, one M. Peter Rogers, a man to whom I am exceedingly obliged for his singular offices of humanity exhibited unto me. Pray use him kindly for my sake. Hee understanding that there is a certaine yong gentleman, called Maister Charles Lancaster, that serveth the M[aster] of the Rolles, intreated me to desire

[1] This appears to be an exaggeration (cf. *supra*, p. 104).

[2] Though Coryat did not live to issue another book, the publishers of the 1616 pamphlet remembered his wish and placed on the title-page a fancy sketch of him riding upon an elephant. This illustration appears three times.

strangers of distinction reach Delhi, they are expected to call and pay their respects to his Majesty, who ordinarily invests them with a "Khillut," or robe of honour. A recent article in the *Delhi Gazette* gives the following account of his actual position:—

"A few days since, the representative of the Royal House of Timour, the veritable Great Mogul of British history, and master of Hindostan, and the rest of the universe, according to traditions which were accepted as realities but a century since, celebrated at the Jumma Musjid (the principal mosque in Delhi) the solemn festival which closes the fast of the Ramazan. Nothing of regal pomp was wanting to keep up the semblance of kingship. Banners waved and guns thundered; and as the monarch's elephant passed slowly along the line of procession, military bands struck up in succession, 'God save the Queen,' while the English present uncovered their heads, and his Majesty, who never deigns to return a salute, reverentially counted his beads. But for the undisturbed presence of booted unbelievers in the galleries which surround the sacred edifice, and the reckless way in which a couple of sowars (horsemen) hustled the crowd right and left, to force a passage for a solitary and unarmed European, one might have fancied that the days of Aurungzebe had come back again, and the English were a handful of submissive traders, only too glad to purchase at any price the blessings of being allowed to wear their heads, and fill their pockets.

"Bahader Shah is really a king; not merely by consent of the Honourable Company, but actually created such by their peculiar letters patent. Lord Lake found the grandfather of the present sovereign an emperor in rags, powerless, eyeless, and wanting the means of sustaining existence. The firmans of the Padshah made the general an Indian noble; the sword of the latter made the descendant of Tamerlane a

Company's king, the least dignified, but the most secure of Eastern dominations.

"In public and private, Bahader Shah receives the signs of homage which are considered to belong to his pre-eminent station. The representative of the Governor-General, when admitted to the honour of an audience, addresses him with folded hands in the attitude of supplication. He never receives letters, only 'petitions,' and confers an exalted favour on the Government of British India by accepting a monthly present of 80,000 rupees (8,000*l.*). In return he tacitly sanctions all our acts; withdraws his royal approbation from each and all our native enemies, and fires salutes upon every occasion of a victory achieved by our troops. It would be impossible to find a royalty more courteously disposed, and as the treaties which bind us to him exist on durable parchment, and are not likely to be violated by his oriental majesty, it would apparently follow that, except at a monstrous sacrifice of good faith, the Mogul line will continue for ages to sway a nominal sceptre. Yet it is almost certain that his dynasty is on the verge of extinction. He is most probably the last of his race who will sit on a throne, and this, too, in spite of covenants and solemn obligations which were to endure as long as the sun and stars.

"To sweep away the house of Tamerlane will not add the slightest tittle to the power enjoyed at this moment by the Company. Outside the walls of his palace the King of Delhi has no more authority than the meanest of his servants, but within that enclosure his will is fate, and there are twelve thousand persons who live subject to it. The universal voice of society ascribes to this population the habitual practice of crimes, of which the very existence is unknown in England, except to the few who form the core of the corrupt civilization of great cities. Its princes live without dignity, and its female aristocracy contrive to exist without honour. The intellectual qualifications of both sexes, with one or two exceptions, do not reach even the Mahomedan standard of merit—perhaps the lowest in the scale of modern humanity.

"But it is not the condition or the morals of the inhabitants of the royal palace, nor the maintenance of an exclusive jurisdiction, that form the chief reasons why the kingdom of Delhi should be abolished. The latter belong to a class of topics with which the readers of Malthus and Poor Law Commissioners' reports are familiar. The royal family of Delhi consists of *twelve hundred persons,* with a sure prospect of further increase every month, and how is the East India Company to support all this army of princes and princesses? As yet the hardship has only fallen upon the monarch, who has been obliged to divide and sub-divide his income, until there are princes who receive only 25 rupees a month! Let the honest democrats of London and Manchester try, if they can, to imagine the case of a king's son, nephew, or cousin, however far removed, living in a state of royalty on thirteen shillings and sixpence a week, constantly addressed as 'Shah-i-Alum,' the *King of the World,* and feeling it necessary for his rank's sake, on choosing a wife, to settle on her a dowry of five lakhs of rupees!

"While this farce of a monarch is kept up, the 'Sulateen' continues to multiply within the royal residence, and to live on the royal bounty, their sole occupation being confined to playing on the sitar, and singing the king's verses. There is no employment for them in the service of the state, and they are vastly too proud to condescend to labour, even if qualified to undertake it, which, as matters stand, is entirely out of the question."

Delhi has one or two broad and handsome streets, a number of handsome private residences, and an extensive cantonment for troops. But the main attractions of the town consist in the mosques and minarets, which are spoken of in another chapter.

Agra, Lucknow, and Hyderabad (the capital of the Nizam), are Mahomedan cities of a fine appearance, from the clusters of mosques and minarets, and other public buildings.

Lucknow is however, more hybrid than the others, because many of the residences of the upper classes are built upon the principle of English villas. There is a park and a menagerie at Lucknow, and the Nawaub of Oude, who resides here, keeps up a sort of ragged royal state, which lends a picturesque variety to the streets. His elephants are numerous, and his guards gaily attired. Of the Imaumbarra and Roumi Durwaz—the two most remarkable public edifices—mention has already been made.

Hyderabad is a very handsome town; seen from a short distance, the rich variety of mosques, palaces, houses, and other edifices, interspersed with trees, give to the whole the character of a city built in the midst of an immense garden. The most prominent objects are the Great Mosque, the Palace of Twelve Gates, and the *Chor Minar*, or four minarets. The town is surrounded by a massive stone wall, sometimes 40 feet in length, and 10 feet in thickness.

Benares is a remarkable city, more eastern in character than the general run of Hindoo towns. The streets are extremely narrow, only admitting of an elephant's passing, and the houses rise above the streets, as they do at Chester. The upper parts of the houses are embellished with verandas, galleries, and projecting oriel windows, with broad and overhanging eaves, supported by carved brackets. The temples are very numerous, and stuck like shrines in the angles of the streets. The city is held in great sanctity by the Hindoos all over India. They call it, *par excellence*, the "Holy City;" and there is a saving virtue in a pilgrimage to the town, and the waters which flow past the ghauts.

Agra, the capital of Akbar, stands on the left bank of the Jumna, and is picturesque without being imposing. It is nearly four miles in length, and contains a noble road, eighty feet wide, descending to the river. The houses are chiefly built of red sandstone, which is procured in great abundance from some hills to the south. Agra abounds in noble ruins; and the most beautiful edifice in the world, the Taj Mehal, stands close to the town. The fort of Agra is one of the grandest in India. It occupies a large space of ground on the banks of the river, and within its embattled walls of red granite stands the Motee Musjeed — a magnificent mosque. The remains of the palace attest the grandeur of its ancient occupants.

# CHAPTER XV.

## CEYLON.

*Productions—Colombo—Trincomalee—Point de Galle—Kandy—Climate—Population.*

ALTHOUGH this beautiful island forms no part of India proper, and is not included in the possessions of the East India Company, it nevertheless deserves notice at our hands, from its importance and its situation.

Lying to the extreme south of the Indian Peninsula, it is 270 to 280 miles in length (N. to S.), and 140 miles in breadth. The land contiguous to the sea is flat, varying from eight to thirty miles in breadth; the interior of the country is mountainous. The former has long been the property of the English, the latter constituted the kingdom of Candy, but is now ruled by us.

The vegetable productions of Ceylon are numerous and valuable. Besides the ordinary produce of tropical climates, no country in the world yields such a vast number of cocoa-nut trees, or such quantities of cinnamon and coffee. The Palmyra palm and the arecanut abound, and are celebrated for their superior qualities. The cocoa-nut trees, which form groves fringing the shores of the island, have been computed at twelve millions in number, yielding a revenue to the possessors of nearly 40,000*l*. per annum. Their fruit and milk are used as food, or for the expression of oil, and the husks of the fruit are converted into coir, which has become a large article of commerce, besides being much employed in the island. The cinnamon of Ceylon, at one time, grew wild in the jungles, and was widely disseminated by the crows and wood-pigeons, who devoured the berries, just as coffee was propagated by the jackalls, and birds who ate the fruit. But within the past twenty years, both of these valuable spices have been cultivated in extensive plantations which are private property.

Ceylon was discovered by the Portuguese in 1506, who established a settlement at Colombo, to this hour the principal European town. In 1640 the town fell into the hands of the Dutch, who for their own purposes had joined the King of Candy in hostilities against the Portuguese. In 1796, when Holland, created a republic, had united herself with France in a war against the liberties of Europe, Colombo and other maritime provinces and towns were captured by the English, by whom they have since been retained.

Colombo is prettily and advantageously situated on the sea-shore. It is protected by a fort, which stands on a peninsula projecting into the sea, and is very extensive, surrounded by a broad, deep ditch; near the glacis is the end of a large lake, which extends some miles into the interior, and in the middle of the lake is an island called by the Dutch "Slave Island." The pettah, or native town, contiguous to the fort is extensive and populous. There are not less than 60,000 inhabitants of a mixed race, descendants of Dutch, Portuguese, and Kandyans. The town is handsome, and nearly divided into four parts by two broad streets. There are many Dutch houses, distinguishable from the English by their glass windows, instead of Venetians. Without the town are many European residences, beautifully situated, especially near the sea. They are nearly all lower-roomed houses, with projecting low-roofed verandas. The floors are of brick, which contributes to keep the houses cool, though much dust is engendered. Chunam, which in India forms so pleasant and serviceable a coating to the floors, cannot be made in Ceylon, excepting at great expense. It is composed of shells, the mere collection of which is attended with considerable cost. The Government-house of Colombo, or "Queen's House," is handsome, and is situated in King-street. The other public buildings of consequence are—the light-house, 97 feet above the level ofthe sea; the English church; a library, well stocked with books of all kinds; the general post-office, the hospital, the museum, and the custom-house. The Supreme Court of Judicature, the magistrate's court, the churches of the Dutch, the Portuguese Protestants, the Roman Catholics, and the Malabar or Tamul church, are, with the Portuguese, Wesleyan, and Baptist chapels, situated in the pettah or native town. Three English judges preside over the Supreme Court at Ceylon, and one of them is required by the charter to be always at Colombo. The magistrates of the district courts are subordinate to the Supreme Court, which receives appeals from their decisions, and the Governor of Ceylon has the power to reverse the sentence of the Supreme Court.

The other towns of Ceylon are—Trincomalee, on the east coast, possessing a large and commanding harbour capable of containing the whole navy of Great Britain; Point de Galle, at the extremity of the south coast; Jaffah, or Jaffnapatam, which lies on the north of the island, 219 miles from Colombo; and Kandy, or Sinhala, or Maha Nawara, the great city, which is situated near the centre of the island in an amphitheatre formed by the surrounding hills, the highest of which is 3,192 feet above the level of the sea.

Point de Galle has a fort, about a mile in circumference, which encloses the town. The houses in general are good and convenient, and the station, though hot, is healthy and agreeable. There is a Dutch church within, a chapel, and a Mahomedan mosque. The pettah is extensive, and is separated from the fort by the esplanade. Point de Galle is the port of arrival for the steamers from the Red Sea, which thence proceed to Madras and Calcutta. Here also the screw steamers stop to coal on their way to the Australian colonies down the straits of Malacca.

Trincomalee is enclosed in a fort, covering an extent of three miles. It has a citadel called Fort Ostenburg, erected on a cliff that projects into the sea. There are a few good houses in the occupation of English, Dutch, and Portuguese, and several chapels, mosques, and temples. Jaffnapatam is a fortified town. The works are in the form of a pentagon, and contain barracks, a Dutch church, and a few good buildings.

The town of Kandy, in the time of the kings, consisted of one street, about two miles in length, having a few narrow lanes branching out on both sides. None of the houses or huts were tiled or whitewashed, except those of the king and his ministers, and a few head men; the rest being covered with cadjan matting, shingles, or thatch. Since its capture by the English, however, the town has been much improved; many new and commodious houses have been erected; new streets have been formed, the old ones widened, and all the houses in the town tiled. There is a pavilion, the residence of the Governor for about half a year, one of the handsomest buildings in the country. The king's palace and the buildings connected with it are now used as government offices, and the former hall of audience has been converted into a court of justice. A public library, erected on pillars built in a lake, is a neat and commodious building well supplied with books. In Kandy are numerous wiharas, temples, for this is the chief seat of Buddhism. The principal temple contains the "most sacred relic of Buddha's canine tooth," encased in a golden dagoba, set round with jewels.

There are several other small towns and villages scattered over the island, but they are thinly populated, and are not of any material account.

In the mountainous part of the interior, fifty miles south-east of Kandy, is the settlement of Nuwera Elia, the city of light. For a few months in the year this is a delightful place of resort. No rain falls in December, January, February, or March, the air is pure and healthy, the thermometer ranges at night below the freezing point, and in the daytime seldom rises higher than sixty-six or sixty-eight degrees, Fahrenheit. All kinds of European vegetables common in gardens grow at Nuwera Elia, and thrive abundantly. It is found to be an excellent station for invalids. The plain of Nuwera Elia is about four miles in length, and varies in breadth from half a mile to a mile and a half. Roads have been made round the plain, and neat wooden bridges have been thrown across a small river that runs through the middle of it.

The population of Ceylon amounts to a quarter of a million, two-thirds of whom are Singhalese, or aboriginal inhabitants, professing the Buddhist religion, in which no distinction of caste is recognised. In general appearance they are good-looking; they have bright black eyes and long black hair, which persons of both sexes turn up behind and fasten in a knot, which they call a candy. In the Kandian country distinctions of rank are rigidly observed by the natives, and a great many of the higher classes now hold important and responsible posts under the British Government of the settlement.

Two or three British regiments, and one composed of the natives (a rifle regiment), but officered by Englishmen, constitute the protective force of the colony. The native soldiers are chiefly Malays and Caffres, and are in an excellent state of discipline.

Ceylon abounds with minerals and precious stones, and is covered with magnificent and highly productive trees. The jungles and mountains are inhabited by elephants in vast numbers, whose teeth and tusks form an important article of commerce. Tame elephants are used for purposes of travelling in the interior. The chase of the wild elephant, though attended with some risk, is a favourite pastime with the European officers and others in Ceylon. A good shot, with a stout heart, will kill a sufficiency of elephants in the course of a year, to enable him to add to his income by the sale of the trophies. A Major Rogers, who for some years resided on the island, is computed to have slain 800 elephants in the course of his career.

English education has been widely spread in Ceylon, and the gospel, under the active exertions and influence of pious missionaries, is being rapidly propagated.

THE END.